JOSEPH CONRAD
some aspects of the art of the novel

JOSEPH CONRAD

some aspects of the
art of the novel

BY EDWARD
CRANKSHAW

NEW YORK
RUSSELL & RUSSELL · INC
1963

FIRST PUBLISHED IN 1936
REISSUED, 1963, BY RUSSELL & RUSSELL, INC.
L. C. CATALOG CARD NO: 63—14502
PRINTED IN THE UNITED STATES OF AMERICA

CONTENTS

v

JOSEPH CONRAD
some aspects of the art of the nove

NOTE

I should like to acknowledge my indebtedness to the several publishers of Conrad's works who have allowed me to quote freely from books issued by them ; that is to say to Messrs. Ernest Benn, Ltd. (*Almayer's Folly, The Arrow of Gold, The Rover*) ; Messrs. William Blackwood & Sons, Ltd. (*Youth : A Narrative and Two Other Stories* and *Lord Jim*) ; Messrs. J. M. Dent & Sons, Ltd. (*Last Essays, The Rescue, Nostromo,* and the *Author's Notes,* written for the Uniform Edition of the Works, prefacing *Nostromo, Tales of Unrest, Heart of Darkness, The Nigger of the Narcissus, The Secret Agent, Under Western Eyes,* and *Chance*) ; Messrs. William Heinemann, Ltd. (*The Nigger of the Narcissus* and *Typhoon and Other Stories*) ; and Messrs. Methuen & Co., Ltd. (*The Secret Agent* and *Under Western Eyes*).

E. C.

I

1936

B E F O R E he died Joseph Conrad had the English public at
his feet ; now it has gone elsewhere and some time may
pass before it takes him to its heart : the empty period is
with us now between adulation and settled regard. Much
has been written about him and a great deal more will come,
most of it addressed to a wider public than can ever be
reached by this study, a public eager to *know*. This book is
neither a contribution to knowledge nor an exhaustive
survey or recapitulation of known facts. It must content
itself with suggestion.

The general situation as I see it is that even among his
friends Conrad is still very widely read, not as a novelist in
his own right but as a kind of exotic romancer who has
made a corner in sea and jungle. With the reading public as
a whole his reputation even as a writer of sea-stories is
diminished, his work too often dismissed with a wave of
the hand. It is my belief that when he is restored to his
proper place, to the front rank, that is, of English novelists
of all ages, it will not be as anything so confined as a writer
of exotic romances but as a great novelist unclassified.
Meanwhile he suffers from his label as other men have
suffered in the past from theirs. His future reputation will
depend, as he himself would wish, less on his purely

descriptive powers, less on the unconventional exteriors of his characters, and more on his skill in rendering life, which is the same the world over, in Marseilles, London, Sulaco, or Bangkok, and the people behind those astonishing façades, whose lives in aggregate are life.

This view is not original. It was offered over twenty years ago by Mr. Curle ; and Conrad's friend and collaborator, Ford Madox Ford, has hammered away at it since early days. It need not, then, be stressed, and although it will be the guiding principle of our examination it is that examination, starting from scratch and made in a spirit as free from prejudice and preconception as maybe, which is the motive of this study : an examination of Conrad in the light of his work, or, perhaps, of the work in its own light, which is strong and which springs from innumerable sources.

If it shall seem that less attention is paid to Conrad's more obvious powers than is just, that is only because more attention than is just has been paid them hitherto. The aim here is to suggest the relation of the parts, conspicuous and less conspicuous, to the whole, not to dwell on this or that detached and isolated aspect ; and regarding the novels from this viewpoint no apology, I think, is needed if those more famous qualities are treated rather as incidentals than as ends in themselves. After all, it is Conrad the novelist we are concerned with here, not Conrad the producer of purple-patches, except in so far as these are integral parts of the whole.

Conrad the novelist—that is our subject ; and most people by now know enough of the broad outlines of his work to resolve any further consideration of it into a consideration of technique. To quote Mr. Percy Lubbock, a pioneer in the game of analysing fiction: "There is nothing more that can usefully be said about a novel until we have fastened upon the question of its making and explored it to some purpose. In all our talk about novels we are hampered and held up by our unfamiliarity with what is called their technical aspect, and that is consequently the aspect to confront. That Jane Austen was an acute observer, that Dickens was a great humorist, that George Eliot had a deep knowledge of provincial character, that our living romancers are so full of life that they are neither to hold nor to bind—we know, we have repeated, we have told each other a thousand times; it is no wonder that attention flags when we hear it all again. It is their books, as well as their talents and attainments, that we must aspire to see—their books which we must recreate for ourselves if we are ever to behold them. And in order to create them durably there is the one obvious way—to study the craft, to follow the process, to read constructively."

That is a dangerous declaration but a very necessary one. Little interest where art is concerned is shown nowadays in the way things are done, in the craftsman's point of view; in most things demanding calculation and severe effort for their fulfilment great store is set by the careless rapture. It is the spirit of the thing that counts, and it is frequently complained that contemplation of the means takes the fine edge off enjoyment of the end. And the novel more than any other form of art seems to be suffering from this refusal to turn occasionally from consideration of the clouds to the earth which shapes them. A fair proportion of a painter's, a musician's, a poet's public is ready to show an interest in

3

technique ; but nobody cares how a novel is made, or should be made ; nobody knows. All we ask of a novelist is that he should be a sincere fellow with something to say which he will kindly say in prose and not in verse and preferably in not less than seventy thousand words. To dwell on technique or to suggest that a given author really calculates his effects is to invite the charge of academicism. It may be deserved ; very frequently it is, but that is the fault of the individual, not of the principle.

An artist, a novelist, has something to communicate to the public, and this communication must naturally be made in the least wasteful, most effective manner possible. And this requirement almost invariably involves conscious choice of means ; " almost," because there are exceptions : on the one hand the rare instinctive geniuses, the Mozarts of this world, who do all their thinking and arranging beneath the surface of their minds ; on the other those novelists of the English tradition who never dream of calculating an effect, who are not concerned with making a direct, precise statement to the reader with no room for misconception in it, but who open the sluices of their hearts and hope for the best.

There must, then, be choice, almost invariably ; and implicit in choice is calculation. But calculation is by no means so foxy a word as it sounds : there is nothing cold in an artist's calculation or the calculation of a great mathematician. Coldness is a negative state, dull and uninspired ; the temperature of calculation in its highest sense is that white iciness that burns, a temperature induced by acutest nervous tension.

The form of a story is, or should be, the appearance of that story presented in its most telling way, and the technique

4

kind of dichotomy forced on us in a study of this kind, is a purely arbitrary process and one dictated by expediency. When form and content are properly inseparable it is necessary to wrench them apart by force, and something is bound to suffer. But it is only in an irreproachable work of art that they are thus welded : more often than not the various elements are inaccurately registered, as the colour-printers say, and when this happens the task of the dissector is made easier. The human body in perfect health is a mysterious entity ; diseased, broken, or otherwise flawed, a starting point is offered for analysis.

It is no longer customary, I gather, for biologists to claim that in analysing the body they explain life, and in art too the only time when the study of technique and form falls into academicism is when an analysis of physical aspects is held to be the key to all understanding. There remains always the celebrated divine spark, and when it comes to assessing the candle-power of that spark the critic must call a halt. Man has measured, so he tells us, the light of the suns, but the light of his own mind must remain a quantity for ever unknown. No instruments can help us here : the light of one man's mind is measurable only by the retina of another mind, of every other mind ; and these are not standardized. In face of this light the critic is merely one of the crowd, his mental retina more than normally sensitive perhaps, but no more capable of absolute judgment than any other. His comments on the power of the spark can never be more than the statement of a personal opinion. And so long as it is remembered that in a work of art the impalpable exists side by side with the palpable, shaping it, there can be no danger of idle academicism. The spark exists, but it must have a setting ; as to the one the critic may offer his personal opinion, as to the other—its excellence, its suitability, its power of displaying the jewel to the best advantage—he may dogmatize a little.

The novelist undertakes to make a public communication, that is his end, and everything he does must be directed to that end and remain subordinate to it. Everything. That communication made with precision, with no room for misapprehension on the reader's part, his work is done.

The fact remains, nevertheless, that in a novel where the technique is exemplary and the form beautiful, that is expressive, the reader has, apart from, or intertwined with, his excitement at the revelation of the tale, an added excitement caused by acute enjoyment of the author's craftsmanship and skill. No matter how passionately the writer may strive to keep himself in the background, the perceptive reader, for good or ill, is conscious of his handiwork. Flaubert of all novelists is called the most impersonal, and Flaubert of all novelists is most read for his technique. This, however, is a consciousness which in no way diverts the attention from the matter in hand, which, from the author's point of view, must be the telling of the story ; it is a consciousness of quite another kind than the exasperated awareness of the author's proximity when he deliberately tries to steal the book by showing off his brilliance. It does not in the least complicate the everlasting problem of the author—how to efface himself : it is a private matter between the reader and the book, and the author is not concerned at all.

Nor is there any reason for deploring it. The highest satisfaction to which the novelist can aspire is the complete engrossment of the reader. If the reader can say, " I was absorbed in your story from beginning to end "—if this can be said, the author has nothing to complain about. And if the reader can add that throughout the length of the book, during all his *immersion* in the author's purpose, he still had half an eye for the means whereby that purpose was achieved, no conceivable harm is done. On the contrary, it seems to me that this dual excitement, the simultaneous pleasure in the end and in the means, is a mark of true reading. Mind and sense revolve in a kind of inverted vicious circle. The excitement, nervous, mental, sensuous, stimulated by the story itself, keys up the whole apprehensive system, waking sleeping faculties with functions of their own, the appreciations of subtleties of execution. And this keen enjoyment of the means itself keys up still further the reader's receptivity, sharpening it to catch the subtlest overtones of sense. Enjoyment of this kind is known to too few readers : more musicians, proportionately speaking, receive this dual excitement from a Bach fugue than readers from a well-constructed novel. The critic can help here too.

In any case the dividing line between what is " done " and what is " not done " in novel reading seems curiously arbitrary and irrationally placed. That vague and inconclusive word " technique " is apparently the irritant. There is something almost indecent about it, as there used to be about the word " leg." Yet many people who eschew it will be as loud as any in their approval of a favourite

8

pressionist approach have been set down with perfect lucidity by Ford Madox Ford in "Joseph Conrad—A Personal Remembrance," a book which provides, by the way, some admirably definite principles for novelists (therefore for critics), but which is chiefly remarkable as a most beautiful portrait of Conrad as artist and man.

Conrad is particularly interesting to study as a novelist in the abstract, as it were, because there was no unchannelled outpouring about him. Like Henry James he was always calculating his effect. I do not suggest that he sat down in what is known as cold blood to calculate heartlessly and with meticulous precision the exact trick he would employ at this or that juncture to sweep the reader off his feet in the required direction, like a wood-cutter felling a tree. On the contrary, he seems to have worked in a state of semi-blindness, calculating as the need arose, crossing his bridges as they came, living, so to speak, from hand to mouth. Calculation none the less, and just as actual as the celebrated Jamesian calculation, the long, dictated cerebral perambulations in the course of which a book was somehow twirled and twisted into shape. It has been objected that the artistic integrity of Henry James could not have been wholly unimpeachable, that in him must have lurked a frivolous spirit inimical to the highest art, all because he once, dictating to his secretary, enunciated a certain God-given phrase : " This rallying of hers is of course the very point, for interest and beauty, for the climax of the romantic hocus-pocus of my sought total effect," a sentence born to shine for ever in the notes to the unfinished " Sense of the Past." And personally, if I could choose between the gift of that phrase and the completion of the book there would be no hesitation in renouncing the larger article. Mr. R. L. Mégroz, in his " Joseph Conrad's Mind and Method," quotes it, the inference being that Conrad would never, never have used such terms in referring to his own work, an inference supposed to be derogatory to James. Doubtless Conrad never would have—not in public, not to his secretary. But in his unuttered thoughts . . . ? Indeed the only difference between Conrad and James manifest in that sentence is that their ideas as to the surface appearance of dignity did not coincide. Conrad was never seen in public *en pantoufles*. That is not to say he never wore them.

And what if he had so far forgotten himself as to talk of " romantic hocus-pocus " and " sought total effects "—in his own idiom, of course ? What else but this hocus-pocus can we fix as the author's concern ? Unless he is of the over romantic kind, referred to above, who regards the unhindered outpourings of his heart as valid in themselves, his only concern is the reader, his only aim to talk the reader into submission, to make him believe. Having a communication to make, the author has no option but to make the most of it, to throw his whole weight into the job of putting it across—in other words, to calculate. It is his duty ; he has no other.

This is certainly Conrad's attitude. In his essay, " A Glance at two Books," which is included in " Last Essays " : " The national English novelist," he leads off, "seldom regards his work—the exercise of his art—as an achievement of active life by which he will produce certain definite effects upon the emotions of his readers, but simply as an instinctive, often unreasoned, outpouring of his own emotions. He does not go about building up his book with a precise intention and a steady mind. It never occurs to him that a book is a deed, that the writing of it is an enterprise as much as the conquest of a colony. He has no such clear conception of his craft. Writing from a full heart, he liberates his soul for the satisfaction of his own sentiment ; and when he has finished the scene he is at liberty to strike his forehead and exclaim : ' this is genius ! ' "

To draw a dividing line between calculation conscious and unconscious is neither possible nor, it seems to me, in the least desirable—to the critic, that is, although to the psychologist it must be a problem of extreme interest. As for the critic—on the one hand he sees the unconscious spontaneity of Mozart, on the other the calculating, conscientious consciousness of Henry James—on the face of it an antithesis of a most thoroughgoing kind. But if he is to keep his head the antithesis must be ignored ; if he is not to be distracted by plausible irrelevancies it must be perceived that although this antithesis does in fact exist its home is on the plane of life, not of art. Mozart's spontaneity and James's lack of it have no more bearing on his task than James's massive build and Mozart's physical frailty. They are facts, interesting facts, facts to be commented on, to be discussed, but facts on no account to be dragged into the criticism of art. All that immediately concerns the critic is the finished work, the intention behind it and the manner of its execution. He can see that a book is beautifully made ; he can point to elements in it contributing to its beauty, its finish, its near-perfection ; he can see how the author has arranged his ideas and how that arrangement is more or less suited to show them off to their best advantage—all this is his material : but on what plane of consciousness the arranging was done, the design conceived, is not at all his concern. His task is to throw as much light as he can on the " sought total effect " itself and on the means by which it was achieved, not on matters to do with the author's consciousness as a man.

The primary end of this study, then, is to see how Conrad got his effects, to open the watch and gaze at the works. About the hand that assembled the works and set the watch going nothing of absolute value, or anything approaching it, can be said. The writer's personal opinion is that there was greatness in that hand and in the mind controlling it ; but a conviction of this sort remains an opinion no matter how many others may share it. And although in the course of these pages evidence will be adduced in support of that conviction, the interpretation of such evidence is wholly a subjective affair. This, of course, is a roundabout way of saying, " I think Conrad was a great novelist, and I'll tell you why." But the purely technical aspect of his work, in so far as it is separable from the spiritual aspect, is very much less a matter of opinion and offers correspondingly firmer ground for discussion. There can be no two opinions about, for instance, the technical excellence of the opening chapter of " Nostromo " ; and that chapter remains brilliant, perfectly effective, therefore exemplary, therefore matter for profitable analysis, even though the individual may feel that the spirit behind the book and the total effect sought are shoddy in the extreme. A wildly improbable verdict, but not according to the law of possibilities out of the question, nor, should it ever arise, capable of disproof.

We proceed, then, in the belief that it is a good thing to watch the wheels go round at times instead of taking the watch for granted as an infallible timepiece. Those who believe that there are no wheels, that the hands on the watch-face revolve by some divine agency, will not be interested. Those who subscribe to the school of thought encouraged by certain schools of journalism and implicit in some such advertising headline as, " Can you write a good letter ? If so you are a novelist without knowing it," will find little refreshment here. And, after all, that is a point of view, and one so widely favoured now that anybody with a streak of democratic feeling in his make-up must seriously wonder whether he has any business to ignore it. I should like to ignore it, nevertheless, if for no more than the space of an hour or two ; and in Conrad we have the very antipode of that. We have here genius, which consists of an original and passionate spirit, hard work, and calculation (calculation, for the very last time, conscious, unconscious, or somewhere between the two). The spirit is an everlasting mystery, the rest we can study with some detachment and objectiveness.

But first, before considering the means, the way in which this genius did things and got his effects, we must inquire a little into the ends, the effects sought, Conrad's attitude to life, to art, to people, and other things implicit in personality.

II

CERTAIN questions seem doomed to stay for ever open, and one of these is how much about a man it is desirable to know for the fullest appreciation, æsthetically speaking, of his work. That "æsthetically speaking" seems to me not unimportant, to-day especially, when, thanks to the psychologists, the study of man has become exact (the word is relative), when biographies of great men sell as well as yellow-backs, and when no biography, if it is to give us the hero as a complete human being, can afford to ignore the apparently trifling fact that while Mr. Blank had a passion for bloaters he could not stand kippers at any price. This kind of thing nowadays is apt to be mixed up with Mr. Blank's artistic produce, a state of affairs arising quite simply from the fact that since we are interested in celebrated lives, and since the celebrated men who most easily capture the popular imagination are men of genius, and since a large proportion of men of genius are artists, the biographers must frequently take artists as their subjects. It is difficult to write of an artist without bringing in his work, and it is even more difficult to bring in his work and not relate it to his domestic life.

To understand the books of a novelist in a strictly psychological sense is one thing ; it belongs to the study of mankind. To understand them in an æsthetic sense, from the reader's point of view in other words, is quite another ; it belongs to the study of art. The difference is real. There is an argument in favour of relating a man's public deeds to his private life ; it is the argument that all matter, dead and living, is linked in a fantastic chain of cause and effect. On the other hand, it is plain that one must stop somewhere ; nobody, I imagine, is prepared to bring the whole cosmos into an essay on the Monna Lisa, and the least arbitrary place to stop seems to me at the frame of that lady herself. Also, to maintain that biographical knowledge of an artist is essential to a proper understanding of his work, *æsthetically*, is to assert the invalidity of every work of art of obscure or uncertain origin. This seems to me a tall assertion. All the facts about the life of Richard Wagner (so extra-ordinarily abounding in facts), collected and arranged by Mr. Ernest Newman, are not strictly relevant to our enjoy-ment of Wagner's music as art, although they do most brilliantly illuminate an unusually interesting personality ; the facts, in other words, do not illuminate the music, but the music itself is a very illuminating fact in Wagner's life. That is all. On the other hand, important and breath-taking as it would be to the student of humanity in us, the discovery of an exhaustive, documented Shakespearian autobiography would not add to our æsthetic enjoyment of " Hamlet "—though " Hamlet " read in the light of that hypothetical curiosity would help us beautifully to a deeper understanding of its author. " Chance," as a work of art, seems no more beautiful after reading the whole of Conrad's published correspondence—but it does, as a human labour, seem more terrific. From an æsthetic point of view the only private lives, the only loves and sorrows of relevance to the reader, are those of Flora de Barral, Roderick Antony, Mr. Powell, and the Fynes.

All this would seem to suggest that the less we know of an artist as a man the better (from the æsthetic point of view) ; that the ideal, indeed, is to know nothing at all. And in point of fact I am not sure that so far as personal idiosyncrasies are concerned that is not the ideal. But here it seems necessary to suggest a distinction between the idiosyncrasy purely personal and the habit of mind alien to a considerable body of readers (and thus, to them, idiosyncratic).

Such a distinction certainly gets over the difficulty with Conrad, for there are a few facts about him which it is essential to know and to appreciate. They are all facts which are common knowledge, but that in itself is no excuse for taking them into consideration. What is more important, I think, is that they are all facts of a kind which might be taken into consideration in face of any author without infringing on his private identity. Conrad was a Pole, was a sailor, was a naturalized Englishman loving this country. Those three facts, somewhat elaborated and with their manifold implications, are all we need to know, and the same sort of thing may be said about any other writer. Galsworthy was an Englishman of fortune, a one time lawyer. Kipling was an Anglo-Indian journalist. Bernard Shaw was an Irishman of Yorkshire blood and nonconformist upbringing. None of these qualities could possibly be called personal, yet they may make their bearers appear idiosyncratic to the heirs of other traditions until their significance is known.

In saying, then, that to understand Conrad to the full, æsthetically, it is perhaps well to remember that he came of a family of Polish patriots and exiles of the land-owning class, that he was a British merchant sailor, retiring with a Master's ticket, and, being a Pole, that he was an idolator of England, we are not dragging personalities into literary criticism. Conrad himself with sure instinct tells us little more than this in his own reserved tale of reminiscences, "A Personal Record." He gives us these three facts about himself, elaborating them at length and explaining indirectly their significance. He also throws in a little talk about his own methods of work for seasoning. But no more.

We have, then, the main facts conditioning Conrad's attitude towards life in so far as environment and heredity can, and by them is illuminated the attitude manifest in his books. The general impression gained from the books is of a man ironic, in some subtle manner fatalistic, melancholy, yet admitting the validity of moods of exaltation— an impression modified and boundlessly complicated by a magnificent temperamental vitality in face of the never-ceasing present. He has been called a pessimist, too ; he has been called intolerant ; but it would, I think, be more accurate to say that he knew pessimism and intolerance. He was a man plainly of subtle intellect which was yet, on the whole, dominated by the heart. His attitude, in a word, was generally subordinate to his behaviour. Thought, a philosophy resulting from contemplation of the years, of the ages, in perspective, may be defined as attitude ; action, arising from a present stimulus, as behaviour. And Conrad differed from few active men in omitting to reconcile his attitude and his behaviour, the disparity between which, in every human being, the strain, conscious or unconscious, is the sum of living, a life being interesting more or less as the strain is more or less acute. Conrad's extremes being quite uncompromisingly extreme, his vitality being high, his life was exceptionally interesting, his perception of other people's lives—this practised perception being a large part of his own life—exceptionally piquant.

His attitude was ironic and (not, for the moment, to qualify too sharply) pessimistic ; his behaviour honourable and idealistic. In speaking of behaviour I do not refer to Conrad's own actions in his domestic circle, which are not our business here, but to the behaviour of the most admirable characters of his creation : *their* virtues, notably honour, fidelity, and what may be called practical idealism, are the virtues priced high by their creator, and this in spite of (or because of ?) his own ironic pessimism. Above all human virtues is fidelity, and from it all other virtues spring. The novels abound in evidence of this belief, and much of Conrad's writing may be seen as a fantasia on fidelity. To save space and possibly ambiguity one sentence only need be cited, and that a direct statement of his own in the preface to " A Personal Record " : " Those who read me know my conviction that the world, the temporal world, rests on a few very simple ideas ; so simple that they must be as old as the hills. It rests notably, amongst others, on the idea of Fidelity."

That much, of course, is apparent in his novels. There

are men like Captain McWhirr who have no qualities
in the world other than fidelity and the strength, the
courage, to carry a conception into the plane of action ;
and Conrad leaves us in no doubt of his respect and admiration. It is the plain statement of what may be called the
moral conception of life as opposed to the philosophical ;
it is unambiguously optimistic—though from it has sprung
much that has given Conrad his reputation of a pessimist.
That is what Conrad himself has to say about life, about the
temporal world, as he qualifies it ; it is an observation on life
viewed as a *fait accompli*, as the boat we are all in for better
or for worse, and with no reference to the shores from
which, to which, that boat is sailing. The moralist disser-
tates on the best way of keeping that mixed boat-load
sweet ; the philosopher speculates on its destiny and
absolute importance. Conrad's philosophy seems to have
been that the boat and its load had best be taken for granted
without undue speculation, which is a denial of philosophy.
Somewhere we get a glimpse of his mind in the phrase
about imbecile philosophers building up a system on the
glimpse of half a truth. There is also a passage in " The
Rescue " which has, I think, a certain relevance : d'Alcacer,
imprisoned in Belarab's stockade, is conveying to Lingard
his view of Mrs. Travers :

" ' No, there are not many of them. And yet they are
all. They decorate our life for us. They are the gracious
figures on the drab wall which lies on this side of our
common grave. They lead a sort of ritual dance that most
of us have agreed to take seriously. It is a very binding
agreement with which sincerity and good faith and honour
have nothing to do. Very binding. Woe to him or her

who breaks it. Directly they leave the pageant they get lost.'

"Lingard turned his head sharply and discovered d'Alcacer looking at him with profound attention.

"'They get lost in a maze,' continued d'Alcacer quietly. 'They wander in it lamenting over themselves. I would shudder at that fate for anything I loved. Do you know, Captain Lingard, how people lost in a maze end?' he went on, holding Lingard with a steadfast stare. 'No?... I will tell you then. They end by hating their very selves, and they die in disillusion and despair.'"

That is not good Conrad, as writing, but most of his philosophical attitude is revealed in that passage. It is the distillation of his pessimism. Pessimism, of course, is the word, but it has little to do with what is called pessimism in everyday speech. And, having got that, is there anything in it to make a fuss about? The attitude is one that must be shared, more or less precisely, by every inhabitant of this globe who does not believe dogmatically in heaven or hell. For all practical purposes the pessimist is the man who leaves the pageant and gets lost in the maze, the Aldous Huxleys of this world. Conrad did not leave it. He took the world as he found it, as a society of men and women, as a place to be lived in, and he made his declaration on Fidelity. He believed with the dwarf in Grimm who said to the princess, "something human is dearer to me than the wealth of all the world." He could also write at the head of one of his novels, "It is certain my Conviction gains infinitely the moment another soul will believe in it," words taken from Novalis.

Those three sayings, it seems to me, are at the bottom of

everything that Conrad wrote, expressing the sum total of his practical outlook. Nothing else is fundamentally important. Conrad has been called a baffling writer and a complex personality. He was certainly complex; in this world the incurable lunatic is the only simple soul. As to Conrad's baffling quality, it seems to me that he was the least bewildering of men and his conception of life simplicity itself. He marched resolutely in the pageant and held to the agreement. He was simply more aware than some that all pageants have an end. Only at the very beginning of his career as a writer, at a time when he still hankered for the sea and was evidently depressed profoundly, did he hover sentimentally round the entrance to the maze. Everything then was illusion, even illusion itself (I refer, of course, to the tales in " Tales of Unrest "). But by temperament he was too vital for that kind of game and soon we know that he has pulled himself together and is back among the actors—not denying the ubiquity of illusion, nothing so facile as that, but simply saying to himself, " Well, of course it is all illusion, what else ? And what conceivable bearing has it on my daily life ? " The pageant is the only certainty, and to that certainty he loyally sticks, for better or for worse. But there is nothing to prevent him longing at times for something better or giving way to exasperation at the stupidity of his fellow promenaders.

I am aware of the dangers of over-simplification, but they seem to me less than those of over-complication. In a world of Idiots (the Dostoievski brand) Conrad would seem a convoluted monster; in a world of Hamlets, Fausts, and Babbitts he holds a course remarkably straight.

As to what was human, and therefore dear, Conrad was catholic enough, and to glance at some of those figures, figures sympathetically described, is to discover fairly soon his own conception of what differentiates the human being from the brute, what qualifies a man to share in the very few human virtues or to suffer through lack of one or other of them. There are fine figures of men of whom he is passionately fond—Dominic, Lingard, Charles Gould, Heyst. There are men who have fallen too far ever to be fine figures of men, but whose striving to regain their footing lends them grandeur—the student Razumov, Lord Jim. Almayer, too, is human. The Professor of " The Secret Agent " is human. Even Willems is human. About all these men Conrad writes with sympathy and all the understanding of which he is capable. It is a weird assortment, but there they are. And to discover the human element, that spark or flame that brings them inside the pale of humanity, which differentiates them from brutish things, which makes them subject to society's laws, one must discover the common denominator of Lingard and Willems, of Almayer and Charles Gould.

There is one thing and one thing only which all these men on their disparate planes of consciousness can be said to have in common, and that is a sense of responsibility towards a conception of life, a passion, in other words, outside themselves. That holds good, I think, for every human being treated sympathetically by Conrad. The Goulds, the Lingards, the Heysts, need no supporting explanation ; but the passion, the sense of responsibility on however low or perverted a plane, is just as evident in those other, more wretched creatures. Almayer lives, however ineffectually, for his daughter ; Willems is never for one moment deserted by his conscience, hopelessly inadequate as it is ; the sinister old Professor lives and starves for the symbolic perfect detonator.

These men are all exalted by their humanness and privileged to suffer because of it. For this privilege they must all carry the burden of society on their backs, but in return for that, even though it crushes them to death, they are allowed to be buried as men. Willems was clever, and had he been outside the pale he would have lived and flourished. But he was human ; he was ruined by his conscience, the possession of which, nevertheless, exalted him above some others.

And those others, those outside the pale, who are they ? We find in Conrad men who seem to be the principle of evil personified ; Heemskirk, Mr. Jones, and Mr. Vladimir. There are other wretches exhibited with loathing : Comrade Ossipon, Schomberg, Peter Ivanovitch, Donkin, Massey, and Montero. And there are one or two characters on the face of it ordinary enough with whom, nevertheless, Conrad shows no trace of sympathy : the rescued Mr. Travers. It seems a far cry from Mr. Jones to Mr. Travers, but this sort too has its common denominator, and that is, as one would expect, a complete irresponsibility, a perfect unattachment from anything but the self, the self of the moment, moreover ; an utter and absolute absence of any scruple coming between themselves and the desire of the moment. It is more than pure selfishness ; the selfish man may be driven to death by scruples which he is too lazy to translate into action. It is anarchy, the natural chaos in which the clearing has been laboriously made. Willems is inside the clearing, punished for his unworthiness. Mr. Vladimir, the hyperborean swine, is outside. He simply does not count. He is, as Conrad says of Peter Ivanovitch and Madame de S. in his preface to " Under Western Eyes," fair game. " They are the apes of a sinister jungle and are treated as their grimaces deserve." The precise nature of that extremely Conradian hard case, Mr. Travers, will have to be decided later on.

Conrad, judging by his villains, seems to have been oppressed by a sense of evil, and evil to him meant an irresponsible force wandering at large in an ordered and respectable society. There is nothing to be done with it at all. It is a perpetual menace, and the only armour against it is a perfect integrity on the part of every member within the gates. Reduced to their barest fundamentals the motive power behind the majority of the affairs rendered by Conrad derives from the opposition of two forces, responsibility and irresponsibility. And the allies of the one are those celebrated human virtues, notably fidelity, which itself, as Conrad viewed the world, is the fountain-head of all the human virtues ; for fidelity translated from a concept into action involves of necessity the smooth and ready functioning of other qualities, such as courage, endurance, decisiveness, humility, self-sacrifice, and so on through the hero's catalogue. Fidelity in perfect action involves the deployment at one time or another of all these qualities, and the failure of one or other of them means the failure of fidelity. That, as Conrad saw it, is what happens. That is what interested him chiefly.

In the irresistible power of evil, in the blindness of fate, Conrad certainly believed, but he was, I think, fascinated by the problem psychologically, not philosophically obsessed by it. Mr. Jones was as blind, as irresponsible, as irresistible a force as the Californian earthquake, and on the whim of the moment he could be as arbitrarily destructive as an earthquake. Conrad was interested in that. Everybody must be interested in it, and Conrad no more than any man who looks with open eyes and perceives the apparent blindness of fate. But there is nothing to write home about in that. What he is far more interested in, what he did think worth writing home about, thus revealing the fundamental sanity of his outlook, is the horrifying spectacle of men needlessly going half-way to meet their fates. Mr. Jones is a menace—well, and so is an earthquake. One takes these things for granted, although it is occasionally interesting to study an earthquake masquerading as a human being. What interests Conrad above all, however, is the subtle twist in Heyst's character causing the loophole through which Mr. Jones does in fact enter. It is the twist that always interests Conrad. The frequent calamitous endings to his stories indicate that he also has an eye for that irresponsible chaos so closely bordering the human camp ; but this is a very secondary interest and one brought into play as often as not by æsthetic necessity. To make the twist clear it has to lead to something, and, to give finish to a work of art, to something definite and conclusive—death, for instance, or ruin. The artist in Conrad triumphs always over the moralist ; but the moralist is strong, and it is the struggle between the two, the artist and the moralist, which, I think, is at the back of a great deal which makes

26

the man seem baffling to many people, which obscures at
times the essential simplicity and lucidity of his outlook.
The moralist in him is too strong to allow the artist in him to
draw with perfect aloofness and objectivity, to render the
bare facts of the case with a simple take it or leave it.   But
the artist, though not invulnerable, is invariably victorious ;
the moralist is kept unceasingly on the run with never time
to point his words.

Conrad, then, was a man with a simple philosophy and a
straightforward moral vision.   Above all he was an artist.
But first he was a human being, and a human being is not a
walking philosophy nor is an artist a retina incarnate, all-
seeing, passionless.   He was, moreover, a particular human
being, a man of sharp intelligence, a Pole, a child of Polish
patriots of the country-gentleman class, therefore of a turn
of mind aristocratic and political.   To guess from his books
that he was a Pole would be difficult ; it is unnecessary to
try.   But that he was politically minded and aristocratic in
bearing is as plain as a pikestaff.   And these are attributes
which may all too easily get at odds with the simple human
virtues ; or, at least, they may make these virtues, standing
alone, look a little dull.   When one is at sea, as Conrad was
for twenty years or so, there is little scope for intellectual
figures of eight or aristocratic feeling.   The job to be done
is simple and straightforward ;   the men one mixes with
are officers and seamen—above all *men*, all engaged in the
same task and few of them cultivated gentlemen of the
landowning classes.   Social classes do not exist, nor are
classes of ability widely differentiated.   Either you can do

your job, which is a common one, or you have no business to be there : "discipline is not ceremonious in merchant ships, where the sense of hierarchy is weak, and where all feel themselves equal before the unconcerned immensity of the sea and the exacting appeal of the work."

Contemplating your neighbours, the only faculty which can in such circumstances possibly be brought into play, must thus be done from a purely human standpoint. They are good or bad fellows, that is all. Plainly in that kind of society the few human virtues matter very much indeed, and, more importantly, nothing else does, or, even more importantly, can give the illusion of mattering. It is a life summed up in the word fidelity—honour, courage, endurance, duty. And when one is a Pole with one's intellectual faculties and social prejudices for the moment perforce at rest, these words must seem very plainly the answer to everything. Honour to the Pole is—honour ; and with good reason. Before England was prosperous and unassailable it was so to the Englishman too—and it will be again in the perilously near future ; that or nothing. And that or nothing it is to the Polish gentleman and to the sailor too, particularly, perhaps, to the Polish sailor working among idealized Englishmen, the heirs to the Marryat tradition. Hence Captain McWhirr. It was required of him only to fulfil, in the fullest sense, his owner's trust ; he needed straightness and a knowledge of his job ; nothing else at all : there was no scope for other talents.

But life on dry land is another affair altogether. The scope for straightforward action is limited there unless one is an engine-driver or a ploughman. The mind comes into play ; the mind of the engineer, the financier, the politician.

28

The simple virtues are a little less obvious. Also one is in the midst of a great crowd of people, very mixed and sharply graded. And in due course Conrad the landsman presents us with tales which are not concerned with strength and weakness unadorned. Complications begin to creep in, social and intellectual, sufficiently strong to upset a man's moral balance. On the sea it is enough to be a Captain McWhirr. But on land . . . ?

That is a question, one of the main questions, I think, to which Conrad's work is an answer. And the answer is always the same. The answer, for what it is worth, is "yes, on land too." But it no longer comes with the direct simplicity, the unhesitating, the ungrudging affirmation of the author of "Typhoon." It comes in a variety of tones ranging from bitterness to resignation. It comes at the end of hair-splitting debates ; it is sometimes plain, but sometimes it is so drowned by cross-winds of desire as to be almost inaudible.

The manifesto on fidelity, which in a moment we shall finish with, is an expression of faith. To some, to the simple-minded, this kind of faith may come without doubt, embarrassment, or question, may come and be retained ; but by an articulate, civilized mind, by a man of nervous apprehension, of predatory intelligence, of finely-tempered, supple intellect, such a faith is not won in a night, or, if it is inborn, is not to be held without effort. There is a pride of intellect, and the power of the mind has no inevitable place among those few virtues as old as the hills. There is too a pride of blood, and blood is not of these virtues either. These things are not subdued without a struggle. For a man of Conrad's mental calibre and breeding that faith, in

29

maturity, can be neither more nor less than a last barricade thrown up against disillusionment and chaos. But a last barricade is not of necessity forlorn.

It is for the biographer to make capital out of this kind of thing, not the critic. I allude to it only as a struggle to some extent conditioning the novels and mirrored in them. As a conflict it seems to me not in the least recondite but inevitable as the day. In attributing it to Conrad one is not at all differentiating him from any other man of acute aristocratic intelligence and deep human feeling unsupported by religious dogma. Yet it seems to have confused many people, to have veiled the essential simplicity of his outlook. This it is, I think, together with the all-important fact that Conrad was an artist, that is at the back of all the confusion. Coupled with Conrad's astonishing intensity of vision it explains that nervous, sardonic tone which, particularly round about the middle of his career, is found so disconcerting by the unsardonic English (I do not mean, of course, the sardonic savaging of certain characters he has taken a dislike to). It explains how this man who writes in such uncompromising terms about various specified virtues will depict a faithful man, a Mr. Fyne, for instance, with a note of smothered impatience, of nervous exasperation, in his voice. It explains the note of irritated tenderness sometimes struck in describing admirable souls like Captain Beard of the *Judea*. Instead of reverence and respect we have tenderness and exasperation; tenderness, the emotion of the strong and ranging in face of innocence; exasperation, the emotion of the supple intelligence in face of the fool and the bore. Notably it explains his reputation for intolerance. To call a novelist intolerant of course is a polite way of saying that he is not a great novelist, but I don't think it is meant that way ; it is a charge, apart from this, absurd in the extreme when one remembers some of those wretched characters, men on whom most of the world would never waste a glance, around whose shoulders this proud seaman, this Pole, this English gentleman of aristocratic temper, has wrapped with his own hands the mantle of human dignity.

And on the other hand we have what Ford Madox Ford has called the " political novels," and political they are. . . . How is it that a man so commanded by a simple philosophy can fail to shrink from intrigue, political virtuosity, and business acumen with anything but loathing ? Conrad wrote of such things with absorbed and absorbing interest, with intellectual sympathy, with the understanding of the spiritually akin. And this is perfectly in character.

For if a man without the ancient virtues lacks foundation, a man with nothing but foundation may be deadly dull. Never did Conrad glorify humanity for the possession of qualities which he preferred to take as a matter of course. He was not one of Mr. Huxley's optimists " who assure us that humanity is all right because mothers love their children, poor folk pity and help one another, and soldiers die for a flag," who comfort us " on the grounds that we resemble the whales, the elephants, the bees." These things we should take as a matter of course. As Conrad saw it, the world in the last resort rests upon them ; and he is chiefly concerned with their absence, not with their presence. His unqualified heroes and heroines are those who did take them for granted and whose fineness is adorned with other more gracious qualities : Rita de Lastaola, Mrs. Gould, Don José de Avellanos, Mr. Stein

31

(what a gallery for a pessimist !) ; and then those fine characters who took their foundations for granted perhaps too proudly and fell unawares : Lingard, Charles Gould, Nostromo, Heyst.

All these he prefers to the Fynes of this world, but when it comes down to bedrock Fyne has the pull over many glittering figures. It is a bore ; but if you make public declarations about the virtues you must stand by your word, and Conrad does stand by his word, his tone at times betraying the exasperated intelligence rebelling against the fact that all splendour without the simple foundation is so much vanity, is as dust compared with the invulnerable dullness of a pedestrian civil servant ; but no more. The vessels of virtue are commonplace and dull ; the brilliance fascinating to the mind is vain. . . . It does not require a mind unusually complex to suffer that mood. There is little trace of that particular bitterness in the earlier books, nor is there at the end. And in " The Rescue," the last but one of Conrad's finished novels, he is more painfully explicit in his simple philosophy than ever before.

As for the subject-matter—it is diverse enough ; but there is, I think, an underlying principle of selection, and that is a never-waning interest in the motives that keep men alive. What is the passion that makes a man cling to life and find it worth keeping in spite of all the evidence of its futility ? And these passions may range from the sheer animal instinct of self-preservation found in a Falk to the practical idealism of a Charles Gould, from the anarchistic conviction of a megalomaniac professor to the exalted sense of self-esteem of a Nostromo. In the motiveless, in those who may live without purpose, he shows no interest at all. It is the ironic spirit in him and the sense of poetic fitness that makes him compass the ruin of his heroes as often as not through excess of those very qualities that give them life.

And this preoccupation with motives (which is curiously rare, considering that we all of us inhabit a world which at a first glance seems pretty intolerable) is the reason for the predominance in his books of characters with a fixed idea. Conrad exhibits no pathological interest in the fixed idea : he is simply interested in dramatizing motives, and he naturally tries to get his motives as pure and uncomplicated as possible. And every motive purified and purged becomes inevitably a fixed idea. To these motives his characters cling as to one firm spot in a wilderness of shifting sands.

III

T H E danger of attempting to isolate the underlying ideas on humanity and the universe in any man's work is the factitious importance that it gives to the didactic element. To say that in all Conrad's work there is no sign of didactic intention would be false ; but what there is has so little to do with the essential Conrad that my purpose in under-lining it is negative rather than positive. In stressing those few simple ideas on which Conrad believed humanity to be based and in venturing here into other aspects of his mind, not as an artist, but as a man, the intention is not to show how much Conrad's works were conditioned by his outlook, moral and philosophical, but, when all is said, how little. Much of the trouble which Conrad has given his readers springs from their belief (a belief fostered by the bulk of English novelists who, in Conrad's own words, are " at their best in denunciations of institutions, of types or of conventionalized Society "), that every story must have a message, definite and clear-cut ; and approached from this point of view Conrad's work, or a good deal of it, must certainly seem baffling.

For although he had very definite ideas on such abstrac-tions as fidelity, although he was by temperament aristo-cratic with an ineffable contempt for all revolutionary activity, although he believed in the ship-shape and despised disorder, although he had a bitter hatred of Russia, as a Polish patriot must and as "Under Western Eyes" declares, although he had in his first two novels and in "Heart of Darkness" something hard to say about the colonizing methods of the Belgians and the Dutch—although he felt, thought, and was all this and much more besides, he was not a pamphleteering fictionist but an artist.

The job of the artist as Conrad saw it is to render life accurately according to his vision. The qualification, of course, goes without saying, since, like finger-prints, no two pairs of eyes are exactly alike ; it goes without saying, and in it lies the artist's entire justification—the bringing of a new point of view, in the most literal sense possible, to bear on everyday phenomena. It may be objected that this is a definition of the aims of the Royal Academy, and the objection is allowed. But the members of the Royal Academy are also engaged in rendering life accurately as it appears to the vision of their President. This means that if their work is to be sincere their individual visions must all have a family likeness to one another, must indeed all be allied to the normal vision of the majority ; to the synthetic traditional vision, that is. And in fact the painters of the Royal Academy are, save by fortunate accident, the quintessential eyes of the mass. The original artist is an individual seer whose discoveries at first shock and then are gradually absorbed into the common consciousness, to become part of the synthetic vision which will be a browsing ground for later generations of academicians.

The very first thing demanded by Conrad's conception of art is the exclusion of all comment *by the novelist* about the characters of a story and the suppression of all personal prejudices, such as a hatred of the Tsars and a reverence for honest sea-captains ; for such prejudices have nothing to do with the apprehension of life but, broadly speaking, with politics, with the social superstructure : they spring not from vision but from thought, again in the broadest sense (all prejudices about, say, merchant skippers, however instinctive they may seem, are, it is needless to say, based on some kind of reasoning). And the artist is a seeing person, not a reasoning person—the artist as understood by Conrad, that is.

Thus in stressing Conrad's championship of those simple virtues there was no suggestion that the dissemination of his views on life is the motive of his work, but simply, and very differently, that the faith we have glanced at, together with a few complications of a philosophical order, is the only element in the novels competing with that purely æsthetic intention which was his one grand preoccupation. In underlining the symbolism of McWhirr I was not trying to suggest that that symbolism was the whole or even the greater part of Conrad's intention, but to throw light on the moral and philosophical outlook colouring all the novels—an outlook which, if not seen to be as fundamentally simple as simplicity itself, is liable to distract the attention from the æsthetic purpose and fill the head with irrelevant bewilderment. Nobody can tell precisely what was Conrad's intention in "Typhoon" any more than in the far more complex " Chance " ; probably he could not tell himself : the main thing is that the story is a work of art, a magnificent prose-rendering of a tropical storm at sea, itself serving, with the aid of the infuriated Chinese coolies, as a critical moment with which to face a handful of human beings, throwing them violently into self-revealing action. The blending of the three elements in "Typhoon" is required for æsthetic reasons as well as moral ones. Later on I shall try to show that the apparent significance of the moral element in this and in other stories is greater than its real significance, a state of affairs caused by the fact that Conrad was impotent unless he had a crisis to work on, and the sort of crisis appealing to the civilized mind is a mental affair, not a physical one, and can generally be resolved into a moral conflict.

A good deal of the trouble, then, is caused by speculation as to Conrad's dogmatic meaning. And such speculation in face of a work of art is irrelevant and distracting. Bothering about what Conrad meant in "Heart of Darkness" is as irrelevant as bothering about what Mozart meant in the Haffner Symphony. Both men were artists, sharing more or less consciously the same intentions. To use Conrad's own words :

"Fiction—if it at all aspires to be art—appeals to temperament. And in truth it must be, like painting, like music, like all art, the appeal of one temperament to all the other innumerable temperaments whose subtle and resistless power endows passing events with their true meaning, and creates the moral, the emotional atmosphere of the time and place. Such an appeal to be effective must be an impression conveyed through the senses ; and, in fact, it cannot be made in any other way, because temperament, whether individual or collective, is not amenable to persuasion. All art, therefore, appeals primarily to the senses, and the

37

artistic aim when expressing itself in written words must also make its appeal through the senses, if its high desire is to reach the secret spring of responsive emotions."

The pontifications of creative artists on art in general and their own in particular are apt to be fantastically misleading, but Conrad seems to have had a greater sense of responsibility than the majority of his colleagues, and with it a mind capable of conveying exact ideas as well as impressions. Most of his craftsman's talk is the reverse of misleading, and the preface to " The Nigger of the Narcissus" from which I have taken this extract seems to me as fine and delicate and comprehensive a statement of the artist's task as any in the world.

The point is, of course, that the novel as a work of art appeals to the senses and must get home to them or fail ; and, as Conrad saw it, this meant that " it must strenuously aspire to the plasticity of sculpture, to the colour of painting, and to the magic suggestiveness of music—which is the art of arts."

There are some people who puzzle their heads about the dogmatic meaning of a symphony, but they are increasingly few. Many more seek to capture the didactic element in sculpture and painting ; but even in that sphere there is a strong party which does not. Those, however, who approach a work of art in which the medium is prose with the disinterested receptivity which they would bring as a matter of course to the hearing of a string-quartet are a most insignificant minority. The fault lies in the first place with the ambiguity of the medium ; but muddle-headedness on the part of both writers and readers must also share the blame.

" The suggestive magic of music—which is the art of arts "—that is plain enough ; the raw material of music has no reference whatever to the everyday world around us, the world of reasoned perception, of logical cause and effect : fabricated by the sense, it appeals to the senses and to nothing else. Ambiguity begins to creep in with painting and sculpture which involve the incorporation of a subject, a concrete subject taken from an everyday world. Even the abstract painting of to-day is not free from this ambiguity, since an abstraction cannot exist for itself but must be an abstraction of something concrete. (That applies, of course, to the genuinely abstract paintings of, say, Picasso ; with the so-called abstractions of a painter like Wadsworth, which are not abstractions at all, but the renderings in paint of the sense images of the mind, as purely sensuous and as divorced from the everyday world of concrete phenomena as the sense images of the musician which he renders in sound, we have something very different, something analogous in intention to music and failing in effect, other things being equal, only because the time element is missing. On the other hand, the *Surréalist* movement, with its ponderous emphasis on subject-matter, approaches the dream world of the mind in precisely the spirit in which Frith approached Paddington Station.) With writing, that ambiguity is firmly and invincibly established. The confusion is between thought and feeling. The question, the only question, is not " what does he think about it ? " but " what does he make *me* feel ? "

Music is the art of arts because it has no dogmatic meaning, no possible meaning outside the listener's head. It can be referred to nothing. A Raphael Madonna, incorpo-

39

rating a legend and human forms, has this fatal reference. A novel . . . well, it is plain enough. Every sentence, every word, means at least two things. It is charged with its ordinary, everyday, literal significance and with its special meaning as part of a planned, evocative whole. The writer who is not an artist is concerned solely with the literal meaning of each word, each sentence. His finished work is no greater and no less than the sum of its parts. But for the writer who is also an artist the literal meaning is not enough ; each sentence, each word must be made to carry a twofold meaning not clearly apparent until the final word is reached. That is what is meant when one says that the whole is greater than the sum of its parts. The process may be multiplied. The ambiguity is generally more than twofold ; it may be sevenfold ; it may be infinite. Even music is not altogether free from this law. Although the raw material of music has no reference to concrete phenomena it comes in time to possess reference to the great body of music composed in the past ; it gathers its own idioms and turns of speech, and these in themselves may be so handled that they bear the generally understood meaning supercharged with the new composer's particular intentions. And so it goes on.

The first duty of language is to express thought and normal values of feeling. In his receptive state a man as a rule requires to be told as definitely as possible what another man thinks and feels ; he requires to be told, but he does not want to be made to think and feel for himself. The law of self-preservation coupled with natural curiosity demands that he shall keep his own ideas while being academically aware of those of other men. His own identity must at all costs be kept intact. In his active state he feels impelled to tell other men what he feels, and precisely why. Neither of these two normal states has anything to do with art. If in his receptive state a man by force of reason perceives—unlikely happening—the validity of another's argument, he may come to agree and change an opinion. But this is done consciously, and liberty of action is scrupulously preserved. And this is what most novel writing and reading with any pretensions to seriousness commonly boils down to. For the average English novelist of serious intention, a John Galsworthy, for instance, whose work epitomizes all the virtues and the vices of the novel at its finest in accordance with the national tradition, is a propagandist using subtle weapons. He is a man who finds himself feeling very strongly about something or somebody ; he examines his feeling ; he discovers reasons for it and dramatizes it in the shape of a novel. Propaganda of this kind need not be confined to a crude article of faith ; it rarely is. More frequently it is employed to influence other people in favour of one's own views about a particular character or type. The distinguishing mark is that in the end there are no doubts as to the novelist's feelings and the reasons for them. Then, if they are put compellingly enough and if they strike the reader as valid, he is at liberty to modify his own opinions. It is this that people instinctively look for in a serious novel ; cut and dried opinions on this or that character which he may agree with or reject—knowing why. On both sides the process works with a minimum of trouble ; the aggressor, the

41

novelist, is never compelled to examine his own heart, for he has need only to blurt out his instinctive feelings, his accustomed judgments, supported by *ad hoc* reasons ; and the aggressee, the reader, follows a line of argument with more or less detachment according to the novelist's skill and eloquence in presenting his case. But it always is a " case." The watchword is " persuasion." The primary appeal is to reason, the novelist's art meanwhile engaging the senses, lulling them. That is the crux. A Platonic dialogue appeals solely to reason (or is intended to ; actually the very felicity of phrasing, of logic, stirs the senses in a most definite way, thus heightening the reader's receptivity) : the argument of the great orator is based on reason, however perverted, his rhetoric carrying on a flank action against the senses. The novelist who is not primarily an artist, every novelist, in fact, with a very few exceptions, bases his appeal on reason and substitutes for the orator's tricks of speech, gesture, and intonation all the tricks of his own trade. In the ordinary serious novel art, the appeal to the senses, is called up to reinforce an appeal to reason.

But there is another kind of novelist who is primarily an artist and who stakes everything on the appeal to the senses, although being human he cannot (unless he is also French) keep reason entirely out of it. He is not concerned with the normal states of humanity, with telling what he thinks and being listened to with more or less respect ; he is not one free man addressing another, each preserving his own liberty of thought and action. His whole justification is his power to break down that stout barrier, the impulse of self-preservation, to demolish for the time being the reader's identity, to overcome all his prejudices, opinions, and

42

notions, not by reason but by flattening all the defences of individuality and immersing the reader for the time being in the deeps of the sea of life itself, of which all particular manifestations are but hurrying wave-crests. That is his, the artist's, reward for voluntary self-immolation and abasement.

He is not concerned with putting a case, with presenting Mr. Brown as an unfairly maligned person or an over-estimated person, but in making his readers see the real essence of Mr. Brown, who is human and therefore dear, with making him, the reader, see for himself something of which hitherto he may have observed only the superficial aspect ; with making him see by a direct assault on the senses, and changing him thereby without his knowledge or consent. For every new thing that we see involves in us some sort of change, chemical or physical or spiritual, whatever it is. Every new thing that we see involves a shock of some kind to the system. No man after he has seen a mountain, really seen it, is the same. A mountain is a spectacular thing with power enough to take aback, to take unawares, to shock into some kind of rudimentary perception the contents of a cruising liner. But Mr. Brown, with the best will in the world, is not a mountain ; we may observe him for half a century thinking of him only as a cultured gentleman with an unfortunate look in his eyes and frayed trousers out of keeping with his lavender spats. The artist-novelist, with his supreme gift, will shock you into seeing Mr. Brown as its mere physical appearance will shock you into seeing the Matterhorn. And the artist, the exclusive artist, is concerned with this shock and with nothing else. Not many of these have elected to write in prose. Conrad as one of them, and whatever pitfalls his human limitations led him into his intentions, his goal, were unquestionable, unequivocal :

" To arrest, for the space of a breath, the hands busy about the work of the earth, and compel men entranced by the sight of distant goals to glance for a moment at the surrounding vision of form and colour, sunshine and shadows ; to make them pause for a look, for a sigh, for a smile—such is the aim, difficult and evanescent, and reserved only for a very few to achieve.   But sometimes, by the deserving and the fortunate, even that task is accomplished.   And when it is accomplished—behold !—all the truth of life is there : a moment of vision, a sigh, a smile—and the return to an eternal rest."

And :

" My task which I am trying to achieve is, by the power of the written word to make you hear, to make you feel— it is, before all, to make you *see*.   That—and no more, and it is everything."

That is indeed all.   Conrad achieved that, achieved it, one might say, in spite of himself ; for there were times when he too called in persuasion, when, for one reason or another, perhaps because his self-annihilation, the abandonment of personality in the moment of conception, was not perfectly complete.   He appeals at times, he must appeal again and again, to the intellect to ratify the vision ; but the vision is always the thing.   I speak of Conrad here, but that name now is the symbol for the whole company of artists in words, even for the sublimely unpersuasive Shakespeare—what did he mean ?   What does " Hamlet " *mean ?*   What is he getting at ?   It will always happen

when words are in question ; and even if the author provides no trace of a handle words will still keep their double
meaning. Music alone is the art which means all things to
all men, the secret of it locked in the heart of every individual (though the strength of the impulse, the impulse to
know, is so unbounded that even into music it is often sought
to read a clear-cut meaning) ; and Conrad who saw in
music the art of arts was privileged in this way to approach
in " Heart of Darkness," in " Under Western Eyes," in
" The Nigger of the Narcissus," and elsewhere, as close to
the spirit of music as the artist in prose ever can. He
baffles, he baffles . . . what about Lord Jim ? What about
Razumov ? What about that Kurtz ? He tells us so
much, he tells us even what he feels if we listen attentively
enough—and then with a sombre smile on his lips adds
quietly that all that does matter in the least. And " Oh
for certainty ! " we sigh. For certainty ? . . .

The lot of the artists of this world is not a thankful one
just now. It has never been that. But to-day especially
prose has come to be regarded so exclusively as a vehicle
for thought, for persuasion, that the contemporary writer
who holds aloof from persuasion of one kind or another is
regarded more often than not as a frivolous monster. In
these days of political absurdity and infinite social suffering,
of unemployment, in a word, there is a feeling abroad that
any man who can use a pen and who has any pretensions
to seriousness should be putting his shoulder to the great
work of awakening the social conscience to this or that
particular and temporary ill. The professed artist is suspect.

The writer sees his tools commandeered by the politicians and the humanitarians, and generally lifts no finger against them. Gifted men who should know better rush in the general stampede to prostitute their gifts for this or that big or little cause, putting their supreme talent to the questionable employment of a prop to this or that attempt at mass persuasion. It is urged, on heaven knows what grounds, that it is the artist's duty to arouse the nation's indignation at appalling facts—unemployment, war, or the slums. The other things, those impalpable things, it is said, can wait. . . . As though there were not a million to attend busily to the problems of the moment, to patch here and stitch there, while only one man, perhaps, in all that million has eyes far-ranging enough to see beyond, below, and the power to communicate his vision.

We pride ourselves to-day on our emancipation from materialism, from the narrow-minded materialism of a lost age : eminent scientists rush into mystical raptures over the stars they are paid to watch objectively ; there is no such thing as inorganic matter ; flowers have nerves and weep when we cut them ; Darwin is decried with shouts of righteous indignation ; the coloured population of the Empire is no longer regarded as so much head of unskilled labour ; big employers divert a proportion of their dividends to providing social comforts for their staffs ; a primrose by the river's brim is—heaven knows what it is. . . . But it seems to me that it has taken a panic-stricken civilization to attain an outlook crasser in its fundamental materialism than anything that has gone before, a materialism which has sacrificed liberty to banking and common decency to oil, a materialism which calls even on the visionaries, the eyes (so few all told) capable of contemplating life steadily and whole, that life upon which the economic problems of the day are but the surface froth, to leave their contemplation and lend a hand with this or that rotten, tottering, less than unimportant prop. And, dreadful signal of degeneration, the watchword is the Mass ; in a sinking ship one is conscious of the Mass and not of individuals, in an earthquake, in a flood, in panic. " You may take it," says Conrad through Mills of " The Arrow of Gold "—" you may take it from a man who has lived a rough, a very rough life, that it is the subtleties of personalities, and contacts, and events, that count for interest and memory—and pretty well nothing else." And to-day the artist is asked to turn from the individual to the mass, to organize a hysteria before of its own accord it has found full voice.

Conrad's view of the artist's task requires no justification, but a utilitarian age must be fought with its own weapons, and Keats, an honest representative of a nation that has raised self-justification to a fine art, has left a most suitable remark behind him : " Art," he observes, " ought not to go about doing good by direct moral precept, but should content itself with invigorating people's imaginations, and trust the invigorated imagination to do the moral good afterwards." That will do for a final word, and anything less in the clouds than that nobody could desire. " Art ought not . . . " said Keats : " Art *does* not," he should have said. As a private citizen and straightforwardly there is nothing to prevent an artist devoting some of his professional skill and spare time to the causes of the moment, thus emulating Milton. But " The Tenure of Kings and

47

Magistrates " was not offered to the unsuspecting public as an epic.

" It is, before all, to make you see " . . . and that can be done by the artist alone. The moral justification, if it is desired, as it must be, lies in the fact that perception, genuine seeing of a kind which the artist alone can stimulate, is the only leverage to which that dead weight of humanity, the inertia of the soul, responds—that state of being which accommodates all evil, which the great German novelist, Jakob Wassermann, has called " *die Trägheit des Herzens.*"

Conrad was a moralist, as every artist must be ; and as a moralist he was more direct than some. His books, as works of art, may suffer from this at times, but they still remain works of art. Never is didacticism pursued for its own sake ; never, that is, is the objective truth as Conrad apprehended it twisted for the sake of a moral idea ; never, and this is the final test, is a moral pointed. First and last Conrad dwelt on the activities of men and women ; his novels are renderings of affairs in the lives of men and women, affairs pursuing an inevitable course sometimes within, sometimes without the boundaries of a moral code —any moral code in general ; in particular, Conrad's moral code. The moral element in the novels, apart from those, such as " The Rescue," which turn specifically on points of honour, is not so much in the stories as outside them. Save in those instances, æsthetically sound, when he allows an actor in the scene to animadvert against specific human institutions or ideals, such as the Belgian notion of colonization, Conrad's didacticism is never, *never* allowed to manifest itself in special pleading either on behalf of an individual or of an idea ; it is confined exclusively to the revelation of a general moral standpoint, colouring every novel and to some extent influencing the choice of subject. Although in a way it is there before us, it is no more than an element in the lens through which Conrad viewed all earthly phenomena, thus conditioning his vision. From the reader's point of view the didactic element in these novels may be likened to a more or less faintly suffused atmosphere shrouding the dead white core of objective truth, to the dust of half the world through which the setting sun glows redly. It is, in a word, a constant.

Once this point is agreed on everything becomes wonderfully plain. Viewed from it the didacticism of Conrad appears different in kind and not only in degree from the proper didacticism of, say, a Galsworthy. It is seen to be, strictly speaking, not didacticism at all, but a kind of philosophical bias. All writers, all artists, being human, have some kind of philosophical bias colouring everything they do. Galsworthy had it, but it was overlaid by his didacticism, which may be defined as the pointing of a general philosophical bias with intent to persuade on a specific issue. This Conrad never did. He was no less free from intent to persuade than Maupassant himself. But even Maupassant, like Conrad, like every artist, had his own philosophical bias ; the bias in this case being negative, however, it scarcely obtrudes. It is the high positiveness of Conrad's bias that makes it so apparent, his passionate belief in morality, that term being used in its fullest sense.

But this insistence on the necessity for morality, while it lends colour to all his stories concerned with men and women moving in a world which, as their creator sees it, can be made inhabitable only by the application of a strict moral code, although it is frequently given point by those stories, never in itself gives point to them. It is, as I have said, a constant. There is never any *ad hoc* manipulation of events. The events occur—as they occur; their significance, their absolute significance, is always implicit in them; Conrad does no more than enrich it with the significance of a personal vision, in other words very lightly to stress this or that particular aspect of the whole which seems to him to reflect more of the inner truth of the matter than any other individual aspect. But all the other aspects are there too, together forming the whole which we are left, without a word, to contemplate.

Not only is there no *ad hoc* manipulation of events to favour a didactic purpose—there is very frequently a manipulation obscuring the clarity of the general moral bias and springing from æsthetic requirements. It is manifest in " Lord Jim," in " Nostromo," and in " The Rescue," amongst other novels, and more than anything else it seems to me a demonstration of how, despite the extremely positive nature of Conrad's bias, the artist in him completely overwhelms the preacher.

Of all Conrad's novels the most didactic is supposed to be " Lord Jim." Through the points of conduct involved in it something of a stir arose at its first appearance, and the interest has remained ever since a moral one. The novel certainly has to do with the problem of honour, but it is not so much a thesis on the theme of honour as a fantasia.

And this fact kills it as a didactic essay while making it as a work of art. To the casual glance the issue may seem unambiguously simple, but really it is so infinitely complex that it can hardly be called an issue at all—not, at any rate, a moral one. That unsatisfactory hero, one may take it, was chosen by Conrad because his problem had to do with the problem of honour which to Conrad was important ; but more than that one really cannot say. Certainly Jim is used to illustrate no thesis : the only thesis of the book is Jim himself, preoccupation with whom necessitates the taking into account in an inconclusive manner of certain issues of a moral nature.

"It is a story," says Mr. Curle, " of remorse and the effort to regain self-respect," and that is probably a widespread notion. Surely, though, that is precisely what it is not. The whole trouble about Jim is that he never does lose his self-respect. He is unshakeably convinced of his own worth. He has been unfairly got at, for in all those countless situations in which he saw himself heroically in action there was not one which exactly fitted the actual situation in which he suddenly found himself on board the leaking *Patna*. He was simply taken unawares, but given another chance he will prove himself. Like the English, he does not know when he is beaten. Very like the English. His very wretchedness springs not from loss of self-respect but from public disgrace. His flight ever farther eastwards takes him not from himself but from public contempt. In saying that " he is a slave to the idea of rehabilitation," Mr. Curle is perfectly accurate ; but that statement is at odds with the earlier one taken from the preceding page. And Conrad himself leaves us in no doubt.

51

At first, knowing Conrad, knowing the importance he attached to the few simple virtues, imagining that here he is giving way to temptation to the extent of preaching, we do wonder about Jim. But it is troubling to find so much being made of the *Patna's* unsinkability. To fit a straight-forward moral purpose Jim's forlorn odessey should have begun at the moment of his jump, *with* that jump, and no later. If the argument is to run as it seems to be running, the whole business of the *Patna's* unforeseen seaworthiness is question-begging and misleading. Compared with the fact of that jump the public disgrace from which Jim's pilgrimage actually starts is nothing. Had the *Patna* foundered according to schedule there would have been no public disgrace, but Jim's guilt would have been no less. . . .

What then? One does wonder a little, imagining that Conrad is indulging himself in a little didactic essay; but the doubt is soon eased away. With the entry of Marlow it becomes increasingly apparent that this is no obvious tale of right and wrong, even a complex right and wrong, but a study of infinite subtlety a thousand leagues removed above the plane of didactic purpose. And soon Conrad himself gives the word which finally proves that in spite of the golden opportunity at hand for improving the hour with an allegorical exposition of his moral views he is here, as usual, engaged in rendering, not in preaching. Marlow is speaking of Jim as he saw him lording it in Patusan:

" ' That was my last view of him—in a strong light, dominating, and yet in complete accord with his surround-ings—with the life of the forests and the life of men. I own that I was impressed, but I must admit to myself that after all this is not the lasting impression. He was protected by his isolation, alone of his superior kind, in close touch with nature, that keeps faith on such easy terms with her lovers. But I cannot fix before my eye the image of his safety. I shall always remember him as seen through the open door of my room, taking, perhaps, too much to heart the mere consequences of his failure. . . .

" ' . . . I don't mean to say that I regret my action, nor will I pretend that I can't sleep o' nights in consequence ; still, the idea obtrudes itself that he made so much of his disgrace while it is the guilt alone that matters. He was not, if I may say so, clear to me. He was not clear. And there is a suspicion that he was not clear to himself either. There were his fine sensibilities, his fine feelings, his fine longings—a sort of sublimated idealized selfishness.' "

After that there can be no doubt at all. Conrad is not concerned with driving home a clear-cut issue, but with rendering a complete personality in relation to his environment—a borderline position if ever there was one. Through Marlow Conrad manages to get in a handful of his own reflections on destiny and life, of which that passage is a fair sample. But such comments are by the way, arising out of the subject ; the subject most emphatically does not arise out of them. They can, moreover, hardly be regarded even in their smallness as *ad hoc* reflections ; they are there primarily as a means of illumination, as an aid to the complete rendering of the subject, which is Jim himself in all his aspects, and in accordance with Conrad's usual methods, methods dictated by psychological limitations, the detailed working of which we shall have to examine later.

The crux of it all is that at the end we ask what precisely Conrad's intentions were—did he approve of Jim or did he not ? And there is no answer to that question—none but the simple, all-sufficing one, that he strove " to make us see." We do see Jim as Conrad, a man of vision, saw him, and we are left with that spectacle to make what we can of it for ourselves.

And this, knowing how positive, how definite, was Conrad's moral outlook, argues a fine personal restraint. It is the restraint of the artist, whose only reward is an uncomprehending stare, and the injured question—" but what does it *mean* ? "

It is plain enough that Jim has fallen. The task of the artist is to show you the man and his fall, not to measure heights and depths.

This habit of embroiling his characters in delicate situations which are not debated to a final conclusion is, I believe, responsible for a good deal of the discomfort experienced by some readers in face of Conrad's work ; and so long as persuasion is expected that discomfort will persist. " Lord Jim " shows us as clearly as anything can that although Conrad was as strong a moralist as you are likely to get, he was less of a preacher than most men. If for a moment we glance at another great novel, also turning on the question of honour, but written at the other end of his career, we shall find, I think, illumination for another aspect of this truth.

" 'The Rescue'," to quote Mr. Ford, "turns on a breach of trust by his typical hero, King Tom." The clear issue with which Tom Lingard is faced (and an issue more horrifically clear, more bleakly devoid of tempting side-paths, it would be hard to contrive) is whether he shall oblige Mrs. Travers, who has upset his balance, thereby letting down his Malay friends, or whether he shall stand by his friends and thereby disoblige Mrs. Travers by virtually condemning her impossible husband and the unfortunate d'Alcacer to death. It is a pretty enough dilemma.

The trouble in the first instance is started by the stupidity and wretchedness of spirit of Mr. Travers. For a moment it looks as if the theme of the book is to be the destruction of goodness by evil. The dilemma is posed by fate, by Mr. Travers (fate, for all its vaunted grandeur, seems very much at home in miserable disguises) ; in the first instance Lingard is an entirely passive victim. Mr. Travers is far from being an evil man in the understood sense of that word ; he is simply crass and irresponsible. Evil is a subjective conception, essentially, and the sense of evil may perhaps be defined as the sense of fear in face of a hostile element which cannot be overcome by the usual qualities of heroism. Stupidity in the grand manner comes well up in the catalogue of such elements. And, although early on in the story Lingard as a result of his weakness in face of Mrs. Travers, together with his excessive pride, gratuitously takes the burden of the dilemma upon his own shoulders, this sense of evil incarnate in Mrs. Travers' husband pervades the whole narrative with an air of fatality. The trouble is started by him, and by him increased at every opportunity ; had he been possessed of a spark of wit, manliness, and responsible feeling his yacht would have been off and away, leaving Lingard to pursue his own eccentric but impeccable devices. Instead he contrives to bring a decent man face to face with his ruin, the woman on board ; and in falling beneath her spell Lingard becomes for the first time an active agent in his own destruction. And this point, occurring so early in the book, is, it cannot be stressed too firmly, as far as argument is concerned, the final point. There is no more to be said and the rest is simply the working out. There is no going back.

This is a point which very few readers seem to grasp, and I hope I may be forgiven for labouring it. There is, when all is said, no particular reason why the English reader of this epoch should grasp it ; its significance is so remote from the normal standards of to-day. But in the understanding of Conrad it is of supreme importance.

It centres again round that question of honour, which for Conrad was an absolute faith, as real and unassailable as the air we breathe. When the breath is gone—*ah ça !* We can all of us say that ; but Conrad, with the French naval lieutenant in " Lord Jim," could substitute for the word breath the word honour. " When the honour is gone—*ah ça !* " That is a state of mind so foreign to the normal Englishman of the twentieth century that when it is made one looks at once for supporting argument. Conrad makes it in his books repeatedly, and we look for supporting argument. But to Conrad that belief was simply beyond all argument, was an element of life, was not a hypothesis or even a conclusion, but a postulate. And this is of importance to " The Rescue " because to the English reader, the average English reader, the first signs of Lingard's vacillation suggest the beginning of the argument, whereas actually they mark the first step towards inevitable catastrophe. The reader notes Lingard's divided mind and his first wobbling between Mrs. Travers and Hassim, and in his mind there seem any number of possible outcomes to the story ; but as Conrad saw it there was only one. And so we read on, wondering, wondering as Lingard gets ever deeper into it. There comes a time when the tension is unbearable, when, after Carter's dreadful little war at the mouth of the river, Lingard (this time aided by the lady herself—most ominous sign) pulls himself together and stands by his word even to the point of taking back the two men to Belarab's stockade. And in our simple hopefulness we feel that all may be well even yet. Lingard still has intact his honour ; he may still be able to save the whites and retain his honour for ever.

But Lingard had vacillated, had gratuitously jeopardized his trust, and there is no going back. It is simply a matter of time and method. The time is not long and the method is dramatic. The final decision is taken out of Lingard's hands. For suddenly there occurs what seems to us, regarding the story as a nice balance of yea and nay, an inexplicable complication. Our interest is all intent on the problem of Lingard's success, on a false problem in other words ; in Conrad's hands he cannot pull through. And so when fate puts a further spoke in the wheel in the shape of Mrs. Travers' interference we are nonplussed. Lingard is inside the stockade negotiating when suddenly, by Jaffir, Hassim's ring arrives on board the hulk, a ring which to Lingard will mean that the game is up, that he must stop trying to have it both ways and decide finally and irrevocably, one way or the other, and that quickly. Mrs. Travers, volunteering to take the ring across the stockade as a pretext for getting to Lingard, fails to present it ; and had her action been made sufficiently convincing there would be in all modern fiction no more awful moment than this. It is thus that Lingard is robbed of the opportunity for making his great and terrible decision : that ring is the final challenge, the imperative, uttermost challenge—will Lingard hold to his word, or will he, under the influence of his awakened passion, allow his friends to perish ? That is the issue, as it seems to us, and by the arbitrary play of fate in that shape of a woman we feel robbed of a solution. But actually we have the solution with us all the time ; it was provided at the beginning of the book. Already when Lingard yielded to Mrs. Travers' spell before the journey up the river he had failed and let down his friends ; for their safety should have been his first and only preoccupation. All that has happened since is no more than the working out of destiny. Catastrophe was inevitable at the very beginning.

As for that final ending which, in spite of Conrad's most elaborate preparation, seems to me to fail, I am not suggesting that Lingard's decision was taken out of his hands for any particular reason. The state of affairs is that the man is doomed to dishonour. Had Conrad been intent on presenting a problem (and to us to-day the question of honour may seem in the nature of a problem) ; had he, that is to say, any didactic intention, the way the book ended would have mattered a great deal. But as things are the moral point of the story, which for us may seem to require demonstration, is taken by Conrad for granted. He is not writing to preach about dishonour ; that is a fact. He is writing to show, amongst other things, how a fine figure of a man may be so assailed by circumstances, by fate if you like, that his very qualities of excellence turn double-edged, so assailed that for a moment he may hesitate ; and he who hesitates is lost.

58

That ending, I imagine, was contrived partly because Conrad had a vague feeling about the fatality of the eternal feminine, but a great deal more because the showing of Lingard's decision was impossible. " There are scenes in life which cannot be written," George Moore has said, " even if they can be proved to have happened " ; and Conrad's instinct, conscious or unconscious, told him that this was one of them. Lingard, while still retaining his honour, had got himself so involved that he was no longer in a position to decide—even if that ring had been presented. What could he conceivably have done ? It would have made no difference, he tells the woman afterwards. It would have made no difference. Hassim was doomed and Lingard's dishonour sealed. Jorgensen would have blown up the hulk as in fact he did. Lingard, faced with that decision, would either have killed himself, or got himself killed, or simply waited in impotence—and the hulk would have gone up. The episode of the ring provided Conrad with what he took to be (and what so well might have been had Mrs. Travers' conduct been in keeping with her character as suggested hitherto) a tremendously dramatic climax, at the same time preserving him from the necessity of rendering Lingard's unthinkable state of mind had he been shown the ring. That, I think, is all the significance there is to that.

As for Mrs. Travers—Conrad needed her to be an exceptional woman in order to justify Lingard's fatal attraction to her. It was imperative that Lingard should be attracted in all his decency, not necessarily because he was above being attracted by a wanton, but because such a lapse on his part would have blurred the sharp focus on the central dilemma.   So for three-quarters of the book Mrs. Travers is glorified, only to behave so disastrously in the end.   She had, for the focus to be kept sharp, to be another Mrs. Gould, but Mrs. Gould would have understood Jorgensen and presented the ring.   The break in Mrs. Travers' character is as false as would have been a sudden transformation under stress of Mrs. Gould into Linda Viola.

The main thing is, nevertheless, that the ending is an artistic device, and the fact that it fails to come off detracts nothing from the fineness of its intention.   The didactic point of the book, in so far as it may be isolated, is that with his first vacillation Lingard spelt out his fate, and the rest of the narrative merely brings this home with increasing hammer-blows.   This may, to some extent, be called didacticism ;   but there is no arguing or persuasion.   The premises are taken for granted and the only conclusion is drawn.   If a man commits a murder in a sort of trance, so that afterwards he can hardly credit himself with the deed— if a man does this and a novelist chooses to render his life during the consequent days filled with the flight from justice and conscience he, the novelist, cannot reasonably be accused of writing that novel to show that murder is terrible and wrong.   Every reader knows from the beginning that the murderer is doomed ;   the interest lies in how he came to commit the crime and in the manner of his inevitable destruction.   Yet it is conceivable that a reader from some remote corner of the earth where murder is still indulged in with superficial impunity might take that book to be an argument against murder as such, and he would naturally look to the author for reasons.   This, it seems to me, is a fair parallel with Conrad's treatment of those simple virtues such as honour and fidelity, he regarding a man with his honour gone as being as impossibly placed as we regard a man who has committed murder. In the study of Lingard the fatality of his act is, by Conrad, taken for granted no less than the fatality of a murderous act is taken by us for granted. He may, being aware that the Latin conception of honour is not fully shared by all Anglo-Saxons, underline a little ; but no more. He does not seek to persuade us about Lingard or any other of his fallen angels, and his point of view, so far as it is emphasized, is less argued than confessed. His didacticism, in short, rarely amounts to more than an open confession of faith of no greater and no less importance in its effect on the story than the implicit confessions of faith made by all artists which reveal unconsciously their attitudes towards life in general. As Conrad himself has put it in his preface to the novel " Chance " :

" Every subject in the region of the intellect and emotion must have a morality of its own if it is treated at all sincerely ; and even the most artful of writers will give himself (and his morality) away in about every third sentence."

What it finally amounts to, I feel, is that Conrad's general confession of faith strikes the reader with unusual force because of its unbending severity. For us it is new, or, rather, unusual ; and since we require the new or unusual to justify itself we look for justification in the novels, finding it, from a dialectical point of view, incomplete. It is incomplete not because Conrad was baffling or complex, but because no justification is intended whether complete or incomplete ; even the little that we seem to find we read into the words ourselves. Speaking very broadly, he postulates the necessity for certain virtues ; he then proceeds to study, to use his own words, " the passions of men short-sighted in good and evil," frequently in particular relation to his own absolute tenets, these generally coinciding with those of his heroes. So long as a message is looked for in Conrad he will baffle, as the lyricist will baffle those who seek logical consistency in his song. But read for his own sake, for the sake of his vision, he is as clear as the day ; his message, his offering, is himself.

NOTE.—Referring back to "Lord Jim"—in this book occurs the phrase, "the destructive element," which has lately caught the fancy of several critics ; Mr. I. A. Richards, Mr. Wyndham Lewis, and finally Mr. Stephen Spender in his book called by it. Their interpretation of it is curiously at odds with all we know of Conrad, and there seems a danger that the words "in the destructive element immerse" may come to describe the surrender of individuality, when, surely, precisely the opposite meaning was intended by Conrad. Stein is speaking :—

"'He [Man] wants to be a saint, and he wants to be a devil—and every time he shuts his eyes he sees himself as a very fine fellow—so fine as he never can be. . . . And because you not always can keep your eyes shut there comes the real trouble—the heart pain—the world pain. I tell you, my friend, it is not good for you to find you cannot make your dream come true. . . . A man that is born falls into a dream like a man who falls into the sea. If he tries to climb out into the air as inexperienced people endeavour to do, he drowns—*nicht wahr* ? . . . No ! I tell you ! The way is to the destructive element submit yourself, and with the exertions of your hands and feet in the water make the deep, deep sea keep you up. . . .'"

IV

W I T H some idea of what Conrad thought and felt as a human being we should be ready to consider what, as a novelist, he did. Let us begin at the beginning, with " Almayer's Folly."

As the first glimpse vouchsafed us of Conrad's mind functioning in private, as it were, instinctively and without any suggestion of *arrière pensée*, before it was assailed by dry-land problems, or by the clouds of doubt which float across the line of vision as soon as any conscientious and reasoned attempt is made to reconcile instinctive ideas with the objective appearance of the world—as, in short, the one and only specimen of his native wood-note wild, " Almayer's Folly " is of very great importance in spite of its spectacular inferiority to Conrad's later work. The Conrad exhibited in this book is the instinctive Conrad as near as we can get, and the unsophisticated artist (not, though, the unsophisticated writer ; Conrad never was that). Later complications and apparent contradictions must all be referred back to this base.

The book is concerned with a perfectly straightforward issue, with a man who failed. It is in intention a rendering of a man's character and the final catastrophe resulting from the flaws in that character. It is about Kaspar Almayer, a

Dutchman, born with as good a chance as most ; he goes under, and Conrad tries to show us how. We have him before us, an amiable soul in many ways, but weak, rotten at the heart. A pitiable soul ; but the artist's task is not to pity, " it is above all to make us see " ; having seen, *we* may provide the pity if we are moved to. Conrad does his best to make us see Almayer, and any failure is not to be blamed on intention but on want of skill, together with the fact that the book was written before he had found the right means, for him the only means, of expression, dictated by his particular qualities and limitations.

Conrad has been called cruel, partly because of the savage intensity of his sardonic humour, but partly because of the mercilessness of certain of his portraits, notably that of Almayer. But it is surely plain that had he been driven by any sadistic impulse Conrad could have savaged Almayer with perfect justification, moral justification, that is. He does nothing of the kind, and the wonder is that he did not ; for there can be no denying that Almayer is not a prepossessing type, and that as a social animal he must, to a man of Conrad's temperament and convictions, have seemed pretty much of an outsider. Certainly most of the world, by no means so exacting in its personal tastes as this fastidious Pole, this aristocratic seaman, would have regarded him as such—and did. But there is no savaging, only a cool rendering of facts, a rendering which fails to move us quite as it should simply because, in spite of his sympathy, in spite of his honest endeavour, Conrad was temperamentally incapable of thinking precisely as Almayer thought, though he staked himself on his ability to do so. It is plain enough that he tried.

He had actually seen Almayer, had dined with him in his fine house, already derelict, had stood on his verandah watching the river at sunset—one of Almayer's own favourite occupations. He saw the man, talked to him, delivered into his incapable hands a pony brought from over the sea, was presented with one of the celebrated geese, "the only geese on the east coast, perhaps on the whole island"—he, a first officer in the British merchant service conversing and trafficking with an elderly, embittered, dyspeptic failure marooned for life in a God-forsaken swamp; a white man—"the only white man on the east coast"—degraded in the eyes of the natives, a standing joke, with not a rag of honour or self-respect left on him, and with nothing to show for their loss. And that man is a human being of the same divine race, a human being with to the casual eye not a shred of the dignity of humanity. Well . . . and what sort of a human being must you be to get yourself into this state, by no means the uncommonest state of all, yet by common consent a blot, as they say, a libel on humanity? The thought of that man, and doubtless others of his sort, haunts this Polish chief officer; and by the process of induction he tries to show Almayer as he really is, the sort of man he is, and the sort of adverse fate that broke him finally.

There is understanding, but no sentimentalizing. There is no comment, neither expression of pity nor of condemnation. The gaze is severe but scrupulously fair. Above all, Almayer is discovered to have a genuine emotion; and a genuine emotion outraged, whether by exterior forces or by weakness from within, is always a tragic business. Almayer knew "the anguish of paternity." Conrad is plainly moved by his suffering, and the weight of his emotion lies above that fatal moment when Nina goes away with Dain. But there is none of that generalized humanitarian compassion to-day. " *Tout comprendre, c'est tout pardonner* " . . . very possibly ; but are we gods to be omniscient ? On the very last page of the book he is explicit enough :

" The only white man on the east coast was dead, and his soul, delivered from the trammels of his earthly folly, stood now in the presence of Infinite Wisdom. On the upturned face there was that serene look which follows sudden relief from anguish and pain, and it testified silently before the cloudless heaven that the man lying there under the gaze of indifferent eyes had been permitted to forget before he died."

Infinite Wisdom alone was capable of dealing with Almayer in any but the temporal sense, and to infinite wisdom this seaman turned novelist never did pretend.

There are three possible ways of writing about a man like Almayer. He may be treated as an object for scorn ; he may be flaunted as an object for pity, or he may be written of dispassionately, as Flaubert tried to write of Emma Bovary. The first is the usual way ; the second is the Galsworthian way (this weak, sensitive, imaginative dreamer broken by the strong, insensitive, and brutal world—Almayer-Falder, in short) ; the third is Conrad's way, the way of the artist who believes that he must render life accurately as it appears to his vision. It is by far the most difficult way, demanding detachment coupled with

66

the power to understand profoundly the actual working of the minds of characters very different from yourself. That Conrad was deeply influenced by Flaubert even before he put a word on paper we know from himself and from Ford Madox Ford, and we can see it in the novels. The power of Flaubert's principles over Conrad all through his writing career and the astounding way (no word less powerful will do) in which he stuck to those principles, justifying them invariably, although his temperament and make-up were in several ways directly inimical to their successful operation, is one of the most fascinating sights literature has to offer us. In " Almayer's Folly," young (as a writer, of course), inexperienced, and ardent, he attempted to take not only the principles but the method of " Madame Bovary " to himself. Later the method was abandoned, but his faith in the principles compelled him to evolve a suitable one of his own, developing the technician in him to an extreme height of competence and driving him to all kinds of devices, among them Marlow, and making, in some way or another, each one of his later novels a technical *tour de force*.

We had better consider Marlow at once before returning to Almayer, for he seems to me to provide a key, *the* key, to all the problems surrounding Conrad the novelist as distinct from the man. He is brought into " Youth " for a specific purpose ; in " Heart of Darkness " he proves his inestimable worth ; in " Lord Jim " he is given his head, becoming very much the author's right-hand man ; and then, fourteen years later, he is called from retirement for the benefit of " Chance." There is no doubt at all that Conrad would have liked him for "Under Western Eyes "; but since even the omnipresent Marlow could hardly have counted a stay in Geneva amongst Russian revolutionary expatriates among his multifarious experiences, the elderly teacher of languages had to be consulted instead, which was a pity.

By some, the sympathetic Mr. Curle among them, it has been averred that Marlow is a bit of a bore : " he is not only a philosopher," says Mr. Curle, " as is Conrad (and a philosopher with much the same philosophy), but he is also a moralist, in a sense in which Conrad decidedly is not." In a discerning idolator of Conrad it is hard to understand this attitude, and to dismiss Marlow in the way he commonly is dismissed, indulgently, even casually, as an aberration on the part of this creator, seems to me to reveal a really surprising misunderstanding of Conrad's aims and make-up, as well as an unnatural lack of curiosity. When all is said, Conrad saw fit to bring him into four of his most important stories, and the simple reaction, one would think, however boring he may seem, is to ask, why ? . . . Why, if it must be put that way, does this excellent and accomplished novelist spoil four of his most strenuous efforts by putting them into the mouth of an elderly bore ? It is to questions of that sort that one expects revealing answers.

Assuming always that Marlow was not conceived out of sheer perversity, which even his hardest critics would scarcely care to suggest, one may postulate as a beginning that he was invented with a purpose, an artistic purpose, one may hazard—not too recklessly, I think. So far so good . . . then what can have been the æsthetic necessity which drove this great novelist into pushing a moralizing bore to the forefront of his so unboring tales ? Evidently a somewhat pressing one. In that case, surely, if we can discover an æsthetic necessity pressing enough to make Conrad " spoil " four of his novels for its gratification we shall have found out something fairly important about his limitations and desires. To keep the argument simple Marlow's dullness has hitherto been conceded, but all that follows stands even if, like the present writer, you have for that gentleman affection and respect. It stands, unless like Mr. Edward Garnett you believe that Marlow came into being because " he saved trouble " (the phrase is not mine but Mr. Garnett's). I hope that in the course of the following pages that belief will die, that it will be replaced by the proclaimed astonishment of a distinguished contemporary of Conrad's, Mr. Henry James, that any novelist should pile up difficulties for himself as Conrad did in " Chance," mainly through the introduction of Marlow. I hope also that by the time we are done we shall, unlike Henry James, have some idea of the necessity which drove him. For Henry James, himself engaged in producing accomplished works of art, had not the time for the sort of rummaging into other men's motives that we are indulging in here.

In the ordinary way to abandon the third person and present your subject through the eyes of a narrator automatically does away with many of a novelist's difficulties (although even then he probably loses on the roundabouts what he makes on the swings) ; but Conrad has nothing to do with the ordinary way, neither is he one who sought to walk round obstacles, as there is evidence enough in his work to show. Marlow, in a word, was plainly the child of necessity. We shall deal with this necessity first and afterwards discuss the obstacles in some detail ; it is enough for the moment to say that Marlow himself raises hindrances of a most daunting kind, particularly in " Chance " and " Under Western Eyes." The narrator in " Under Western Eyes " is not Marlow, of course ; but for the purposes of this inquiry he may legitimately be counted in. (That elderly teacher of languages, the friend of Miss Haldin's, does not supply his name, but one may guess that it also was Marlow ; a brother of the retired deep-water sailor, perhaps, or certainly a first cousin.) For the moment, however, the conclusion is that Marlow was invented to enable his creator to do certain things which he could not otherwise have done. And since only two things could have prevented Conrad from doing what he wished, Marlow is plainly there to overcome one or other of them, probably both. These two things are, first his ideals as an artist, and secondly, his limitations as an artist. The most obvious way to discover the true inwardness of Marlow and at the same time of Conrad, is to consider his functions in the books he appears in and to refer back to a book belonging to the pre-Marlow period, say " Almayer's Folly," or " An Outcast of the Islands," or " The Nigger of the Narcissus."

The most obvious thing that Marlow does is to moralize (to use Mr. Curle's word) ; he moralizes about Youth, about Captain Beard, about Kurtz, about Tuan Jim, about the whole gallery of " Chance "—the de Barrals, the Fynes, Captain Antony, the wicked governess and all ; and in "Under Western Eyes" his brother—or his cousin—moralizes with gusto about Russia and revolutionaries and all the individuals he runs into. Assuming for the moment the truth of that statement, that " Marlow moralizes in a sense in which Conrad decidedly does not," suggesting that Marlow's reflections are not really Conrad's reflections at all, it still tells us nothing ; for Conrad was inhibited from moralizing openly and whole-heartedly, as Marlow does, by his own æsthetic ideals, by the Flaubertian principle that the author must keep outside his story. Had Conrad started moralizing about Almayer as Marlow moralizes about Jim, he would irretrievably have shattered his convention, the basis of his illusion—that convention which demands complete aloofness on the part of the author. It would have involved his stepping into the frame with results as destructive to illusion as Thackeray ever achieved, and in a manner which would have made poor Flaubert turn in his grave—as he probably did at certain passages in " Almayer's Folly."

Conrad, as author, was inhibited from introducing his own comments on men and affairs, yet we find Marlow moralizing with ease, fluency, and conviction. We find, moreover, that his capacity for moralizing is quite half the justification for his existence ; we find that his reflections and discursive comments on characters and events are responsible for a great part of their life, reality, and vividness. In view of this it is surely not too reckless to conclude that Conrad himself approved of those reflections, even that he himself felt the need of them for the proper realization of his story, and thus, prevented himself from making them, hit on Marlow as a technical device to enable him, the author, to introduce his own observations, to moralize freely, without breaking into the frame of the story.

Thus far one arrives still leaving the validity of that statement (about the difference between Marlow and Conrad) unquestioned, when in fact it seems to me extremely questionable.

It is true enough to say that there is a difference between Marlow's and Conrad's moralizing, but it is only one of style. Although Marlow is a technical device and Conrad's right-hand man, he is not a puppet, a ventriloquist's doll. Conrad never concerned himself with puppets. This perambulating and much travelled technical device is a character as real as any other, with flesh, blood, mannerisms, idiosyncrasies, and private turns of thought, a man who can get up and walk of his own free will to lead a continued existence beyond the covers of a book, just as any other successful character in Conrad. He has only one thing in common with his creator, but that for our purposes is all-important ; he shared his fundamental outlook on life. Marlow as essayist would have a style somewhat different from Conrad as essayist, but faced with the same subject the matter of their observations and the nature of their conclusions would be much the same. In that sense, and in that sense only, does Marlow moralize as Conrad decidedly does not. Mr. Curle, I am sure, did not mean his statement to be interpreted literally, but read in any other way it does not hold water. Had " Lord Jim " been the only book containing Marlow the reader would have less grounds for assuming that Marlow and Conrad are one, for here, more than in any other novel, Marlow appears as an active character, not simply as a narrator and receiver of

72

confidences. Judging from " Lord Jim " alone, one might assume, perhaps, that Marlow was a character under observation just as much as Jim or the President of the Court of Inquiry ; but the evidence of " Youth," " Heart of Darkness," " Chance," and " Under Western Eyes " (to say nothing of the indirect evidence of every other novel Conrad wrote—to be considered later) positively drives us to the conclusion that, as an observed character, Marlow is *hors de concours*. He is Conrad. Had Conrad wished to disassociate himself from Marlow's pronouncement he would have been bound to treat him on the same terms as any other character in the novels, and this he did not do. Finally, in " A Personal Record," in " The Mirror of the Sea," and in a considerable number of essays Conrad does comment, or moralize, on everything that crops up with a whole-heartedness that would have done credit to Marlow himself. The moralizing in " The Secret Agent " is very different in tone from the moralizing of Marlow ; it is just as fluent, nevertheless, and the tone, as we shall see later, was imposed by that same æsthetic necessity which lies behind the genesis of Marlow.

Marlow was invented so that Conrad could moralize (and here I should like to substitute the word " comment " for " moralize," and adhere henceforward to this substitution) freely without ruining his illusion, the illusion which was dependent on his, the author's, aloofness and impersonality. That much we have got. But by far the most interesting half of the question, that initial " why ? " still lies before us. . . . Why, it runs, did Conrad want to

73

comment on his characters at all ? . . . It is a nasty question indeed, a leading question if ever there was one, and one that puts the immediate Marlow problem in the shade. To find an answer we must return to that fountain-head of Conrad's inspiration, Kaspar Almayer.

It is hardly, I imagine, a statement of purely personal opinion to say that Almayer is one of the most poorly realized figures in the whole of Conrad. He does not come alive, if ever he comes alive, until the last phase of the story ; and if we look closely the reason is plain enough to see.

Possibly some readers will object to this criticism. It is naturally relative : compared with the characters of most novels Almayer is very much alive, but such a comparison brings us nowhere : the relevant one is with Lord Jim, Captain Beard, Lingard, Nostromo, or any other central character in any of the novels. Almayer is the central figure of his book just as Jim is of his ; and if the one is not as real, as vivid, as the other, a certain degree of failure is indicated. A different objection might be that Lord Jim himself is a very definite sort of character, while Almayer, temperamentally vague and shadowy, could not be realized with such sharpness of definition. But this, apart from all other arguments against it, is contradicted in the most effective possible way by Conrad himself. Writing elsewhere he has left us a portrait of Almayer of a definition as sharp as could be desired. In those few pages of " A Personal Record " in which Conrad describes his first meeting with Almayer there is a portrait durable, complete, and almost painfully alive. In a handful of apparently casual sentences Almayer is " got in " as he is never got

74

in in all the pages of his own two novels put together, and as unforgettably as any character in the later novels.

Finally, and most plausibly, it may be objected that this being Conrad's first book one cannot expect perfection ; and nor can one. It goes without saying that had he been more at home with his medium Conrad would have cut a better figure with his first hero. In a first book, as you so justly remark, one does not expect the last word in technical dexterity ; but apart from deficiencies due to lack of practice a first book is as often as not the school in which a novelist learns his limitations, his strength, and his weakness ; and I think we shall find that the comparative ineffectiveness of that obscure character who made so powerful an effect on this obscure sailor that in his late thirties he was impelled to write a book about him was due as much to Conrad's permanent limitations as to his lack of technical skill, limitations which, as we shall see, he later made a virtue of with brilliant success. Almayer is not a failure because Conrad at the time of his conception could not draw a vivid character ; the living quality of Lakamba and Babalatchi in that story are witness enough to that. Almayer's lifelessness is due to another cause.

What, after all, does the book tell us about the man ? A few abstract things about his make-up, things which apply equally well to hundreds of people all over the world ; but little more. He is rendered as weak, ambitious, lazy, shiftless, sensitive, incapable—a characterless dreamer, in short, with the one redeeming passion of his love for Nina his daughter. This much we are offered, but there is

75

little or nothing to fix the man as an individual unmistakable and unique. Nothing, that is, until the end when, too late, much too late, we do get a glimpse or two of a *man*, an individual emerging with inimitable characteristics from the nebulous background of his type. I instance the little scene in which he is lying drunk after the departure of the naval officers. And then, finally, immediately after the climax of the book (but not during it ; he is still a stick there), when Dain has carried Nina away for ever, the man does spring to our eyes with an almost sickening reality, and for the first time he is a man of flesh and blood, an unmistakable individual—the same individual, moreover, as the man we are to meet later in " A Personal Record." Almayer and his servant, Ali, have watched out of sight the sail of the boat bearing Nina irrevocably away. Almayer stands without moving. Ali grows anxious :

" ' Master,' he said timidly, ' time to get house now. Long way off to pull. All ready, sir.'

" ' Wait,' whispered Almayer.

" Now she was gone his business was to forget, and he had a strange notion that it should be done systematically and in order. To Ali's great dismay he fell on his hands and knees, and creeping along the sand erased carefully with his hand all traces of Nina's footsteps. He piled up small heaps of sand, leaving behind him a line of miniature graves right down to the water. After burying the last slight imprint of Nina's slipper he stood up, and, turning his face towards the headland where he had last seen the prau, he made an effort to shout out loud again his firm resolve never to forgive. Ali watching him uneasily saw only his lips move, but heard no sound. He brought his

76

foot down with a stamp. He was a firm man—firm as a rock. Let her go. He never had a daughter. He would forget. He was forgetting already."

That is Almayer, and that is—Conrad.

In this first book we are provided with a pretty complete history of Almayer's life, with special stress on his fatal mistake, that of marrying for money Lingard's protégée from the pirate ship. We are shown all this, however, in retrospective narrative, in swift, bald narrative at that, arising from Almayer's train of thought as he stands at sunset on his verandah watching the flood waters swirl past Sambir on the way to the sea. Conrad has got his history well enough and as the history of a given man it is perfectly convincing, as all Conrad's histories are ; plenty of men have come to grief through marrying for money in the naïve hope that they will be able to make other arrangements later on. Plenty of men have been flaccid enough to allow a stronger personality to tamper with their fates. And that is the core of the trouble : plenty of men have . . . and Almayer only one of them. To rely for your portrait on an enumeration of qualities, incidents and accidents that may be found in the lives of many other men is fatal. The image evoked is of a type, not of a person.

If a novelist proposes to avoid describing his chief character externally (and all we know of Almayer is that he is large and, from the last page, that he favoured a beard) and desires to build him up from within, as it were, it is plain that he must have a very complete knowledge and understanding of the inside. It is not enough to describe fleetingly commonplace situations in which he finds himself (and the situations in " Almayer's Folly " are essentially commonplace, lent distinction only by the oriental trappings) and to indicate, also fleetingly, his generalized commonplace reactions to those situations. What is required is a revelation of the precise thoughts and turns of thought (turns of thought above all, perhaps) of that character, not only at critical moments but also in moments of relaxation. If this is not done he must be fixed firmly, and in fewer words and more dramatically, by being placed in particular scenes, which may be commonplace in themselves, the individual and finally characteristic points of his speech, gestures, and behaviour being emphasized. An example of the one method is the interior monologue which Conrad attempted unsuccessfully at the beginning of " Almayer " ; an example of the second is that brief but all-illuminating scene which we have just quoted. For although a man's idiosyncrasies of behaviour, his gestures, his turns of thought, and so on, may in the absolute be of small importance beside the root and fundamental motives ruling him, they alone have the power to crystallize the amorphous and inarticulate body of his general state of mind. To emphasize the general character of a man's mentality is not enough (that is the historian's task) ; it must be revealed by its particular manifestations, distilled in a memorable gesture, as Conrad revealed Almayer, too late, in that superb little scene on the beach.

But for the bulk of the book his faith is pinned to Almayer's swift, retrospective train of thought. Conrad does not gaze at him and paint what is clear to his eye and plain to his ear ; he banks on the man's revealing himself through his own thoughts. The result is a blur. On the other hand, when the one-eyed statesman Babalatchi comes on to the scene he is rendered mainly from without (actually Conrad mixes his methods in a most unsatisfactory and novice-like way, but the emphasis is on the exterior presentation). He is given as seen through a pair of human eyes, this involving a definite angle of vision. And Babalatchi, as most people must agree, is highly successful for what he is worth. Had Almayer been treated in that way too he also would have been successful. But he is not. We are given not a compact, self-contained figure seen by a second person but an embodied consciousness. He is never described from the outside and his reflections are offered as they are alleged to pass through his mind ; his speech is offered as so many words in such and such a tone of voice, and out of the gradual accumulation of these reflections and speeches the man is supposed to build himself up before our wondering eyes.

But what in fact happens ? All that we know of the man when that retrospect on which Conrad banks so much begins is that he indulges freely in dreams of a splendid future which is bound up with the influx of problematical gold desired chiefly for the sake of his daughter and for relief from the present reality, unspecified, which he finds intolerable ; we have a certain type of man, but that is all ; he may be anybody yet. And then, after that poor little close-up, which is Conrad's so earnest attempt to emulate *la casquette de Charbovari* (we may surely laugh a little when we remember the undreamt-of heights to which Conrad later soared ? we may perhaps at last cease to take this first novel seriously, if only in deference to Conrad's mature achievement ?), we are rushed away to begin the elaborate particularization of these interesting scraps of news. In

79

retrospect we come to learn the precise cause of the intolerableness of the present reality, the material basis of Almayer's continued hopefulness, and a few things more of a like kind ; we have in short learnt all there is to know about Almayer's personal history and something of the sort of man he is : but as to the actual man hardly a word. And then in a breath the story is launched. Almayer, so inadequately though so lengthily got in, is shunted on to a side-line while Conrad spreads himself rapturously on Nina and the Malays. He reappears with effect only when the plot is laid and his calamity imminent. The greater part of the book in fact is not about Almayer at all, but about the concatenation of events, outside his knowledge and sphere of influence, which caused his final catastrophe.

Yet the book is called " Almayer's Folly," not " Nina's Victory," and Conrad was haunted by the man for years. He was so gripped by him that he set off to write a psychological study of him in the manner of " Madame Bovary," Flaubert's method of revealing Emma probably seeming to him, the 'prentice hand, the only truly satisfactory way. He set out, that is, employing a method which demands an absolute and intimate insight into the mind of the character to be portrayed at every phase of its existence, the power of psychological analysis most highly developed, the power not only to sympathize acutely with another person of a temperament and make-up foreign to your own, but also to enter precisely into the minutiæ of his thoughts, emotions, and sensations. It is a method which has proved a heavy cross to some of the greatest of its exponents, and which as a rule is used only by novelists discussing themselves under an assumed name. Conrad, however, never indulged in autobiographical fantasy in that sense; when he does appear in his own stories, as in " The Shadow Line " or " The Arrow of Gold," it is always as an active figure not to be discussed but to be touched in. In " Almayer's Folly " the man he set out to discuss was as dissimilar to himself as Emma Bovary was to Flaubert; he was simply a man for whom he felt an active sympathy, of whose tragi-comic fate he was emotionally aware. Of him he could say—" Ah ! I can *see* . . . ! " and so in a measure could we all. How often we say, " I can understand precisely how he came to do it ! " when speaking of some piece of conduct frowned on by others. Yet what does such " understanding " really amount to ? It is surely no more than a moment of acute, exalted sympathy ; it is a kind of emotional wave sweeping over the consciousness, obliterating for a moment its accustomed landmarks and for a moment suggesting the human soul in its unmoulded state, a ground from which all things may spring, unwritten on by habit and experience. But when we attempt to arrest the moment, to view, as it were, the terrain in cold daylight, to arrive, starting from spiritual anarchy, step by step at the precise construction of an act, a mental gesture, a state of mind, of the consciousness which will behave in a certain way under a given stimulus—well, habit and experience are too much for us. Flaubert, Henry James, Ford Madox Ford, among others, have ventured bravely into that waste, the raw material of the consciousness, reconstructing sometimes with success and sometimes not. Conrad, setting out to reveal Almayer's consciousness, never began that enterprise : he experienced the wave of

hook let down from a vessel exploring the ocean-bed ; but he never does more than this. And of extreme importance is the fact that such incursions invariably occur when the character under observation has all his defences down and is simply Man in face of catastrophe. They are, moreover, nearly always the outcome of urgent technical necessity, the need for sudden dramatic revelation or for getting the story along at an accelerated pace. For nine-tenths of the time the outside view suffices.

If this suggests anything at all it is that Conrad saw the weakness of his early attempts at the interior method of presentation, and, realizing his temperamental incapacity to glorify that method, turned his back on it for ever. The suggestion is there, but the proof is lacking. Had we no more than that to go on we should never be finally justified in concluding that this avoidance of the interior method was compelled by necessity : for all we could say to the contrary Conrad might have been a regular dab at it, taking to the outside view simply because he preferred it. Happily it is by no means all, for those early novels were written, and also the volume called " Tales of Unrest." We still have his very first novel of all, the school in which he discovered his limitations and his strength. And the fact that in " Almayer's Folly " he did try the interior method only to make a hash of it—that, coupled with the second fact that after a half-hearted attempt in " An Outcast of the Islands " he never put his hand to it again, suggests, I think with some conclusiveness, that this was not his method.

To clinch the matter, to give it a final twist, we have also " Tales of Unrest," a volume of stories chiefly remarkable for the only tale of Conrad's which practically all his admirers agree to call a failure, that interminable and embarrassing fiasco called " The Return." This story purports to be what would nowadays be called the interior monologue of a respectable and empty business man faced with the desertion of his no less respectable and empty wife. It is a failure for precisely that reason, as anybody heroic enough to read the thing through can see. Conrad in his own splendid way was perfectly capable of getting Alvan Hervey in and of making him live before our eyes to be intimately understood by us ; but in fact he goes about it not in his own way but in another's, with results disastrous. His own remarks on this story are both illuminating and to the point. In a letter to Mr. Garnett he writes : " ' The Return ' is as false as a sermon by an Archbishop," and in the preface to " Tales of Unrest," written a quarter of a century after their first publication, he is more specific :

" I don't want to talk disrespectfully about any pages of mine. Psychologically there were no doubt good reasons for my attempt ; and it was worth while, if only to see of what excesses I was capable in that sort of virtuosity. In this connection I should like to confess my surprise on finding that notwithstanding all its apparatus of analysis the story consists for the most part of physical impressions ; impressions of sound and sight, railway station, streets, a trotting horse, reflections in mirrors, and so on, rendered as if for their own sake and combined with a sublimated description of a desirable middle-class town-residence which somehow manages to produce a sinister effect."

Later on it may be useful to come back to that passage, but for the moment it is enough to establish that after

" The Return," apart from the half-hearted attempt in the Almayer-Willems book, Conrad never again set up " the apparatus of analysis." Never. And since this apparatus is the apparatus *par excellence* of the natural psychologist there is surely every reason for concluding that Conrad was not a natural psychologist, an analytical psychologist like the majority of his greatest colleagues, past and present.

We come here at once into difficulties for lack of proper terms. In the generally understood sense of the word we are all of us to some extent psychologists, and Conrad was supreme—in the generally understood sense of the word. He was not, however, a psychologist in the sense that Henry James, Maupassant, or Flaubert were, or that Ford Madox Ford is to this day, and we shall have to find words and a formula to make this difference clear. For the moment, and without committing ourselves further, it will suffice to say that Conrad was temperamentally incapable of revealing *objectively* (that word thrice underlined) the train of thought of a character alien to himself. In his own way he could give us Emma Bovary as vividly as Flaubert, but not in Flaubert's way ; in his own way he could have given us Tietjens, Macmaster, and Valentine Wannop as well as Ford, but not in Ford's way ; in his own way he could have given us Leopold Bloom as well as Joyce, but not in Joyce's way. He could never, as these three writers did, have given us a sustained vision of the world seen through the eyes of these characters together with all their hidden thoughts objectively recorded. His way is to show us the characters from the outside until we see them so vividly and in a light, or a variety of lights, so significant and revealing that their souls are naked before our eyes ; and with that he will comment *subjectively* about their motives, thoughts, and general states of mind. That is plainly necessary, for broadly speaking the only alternative to the interior monologue in some form or other is the sharp-imaging of externals and subjective guesswork, openly proclaimed as such. And here, if you believe with all the novelists of the great tradition in objectivity, in the impersonality of the author, is the difficulty, the impossible difficulty. For comment is forbidden, all subjective reflection on the part of the author is wholly out of the question. And this leaves you with two alternatives. First you may write very much as a dramatist writes, describing your characters and their activities in the third person always from the outside and making them give themselves away with their own speech and gestures. This is sometimes an admirable method, but it is not wholly satisfactory if you are more concerned, as Conrad was, with mental and spiritual atmosphere than the clear-cut facts of thought and feeling. Conrad employed it very successfully in " Nostromo " up to a point, but even then he had to call in his habitual devices for help at times. In the second place you may write in the first person as an actor in the story, as Conrad did in " The Arrow of Gold," " The Shadow Line," and various short stories, a method which allows great freedom of movement but has serious drawbacks to be considered later. Thirdly, you may make a character in the story relate and comment as you, the author, would yourself were you not vowed to aloofness and objectivity. This method is also used for other reasons than inability to work in any other way. Henry James employed it as a most suitable method for getting a variety of points of view on a central situation. But Conrad employed it because he was a subjective visionary committed to the ideal of objectivity. Hence, to return abruptly to our leading question, Marlow (seen no longer to be a whim but a matter of sternest necessity) ; a character whom, with Mr. Curle, you are at liberty to condemn, but only on the understanding that with him you damn Conrad too. Hence Marlow—and with him the first person singular, and the elderly teacher of languages, and Martin Decoud, and, even more subtly, the ironic method of " The Secret Agent," and a crowd of other more mechanical devices.

We have spoken of what Conrad could and could not do, but we cannot get away with it as easily as that. We have got an answer to our Marlow question, but before it can be allowed to stand we shall have to go a little more explicitly into this business of psychology.

V

CONRAD'S propensity for serving up in the form of fiction actual experiences lived by himself or heard of at second-hand is well known ; but to me it seems to be a fact of extreme significance and one going hand in hand with what we have so far called his psychological limitations, possibly even springing directly from the cause of these. Because of this I make no apology for dwelling at some length on a point which by most writers on Conrad is casually mentioned and let pass. That he frequently drew from life is well known, but few of his readers, I imagine, are aware that he rarely, if ever, did anything else. There is, as far as one can gather, hardly a single invented character in the whole of his output. To no book could he honestly have fixed the conventional disclaimer that " the characters in this story are entirely imaginary." And it is the same with situations. Although he manipulated situations, combined them for dramatic effect, piled agony on agony by putting a single character through a series of situations in real life shared more modestly by a number of different men, his inventive faculty was as incapable of fabricating wholly imaginary situations as wholly imaginary characters.

All novelists to a greater or less degree base their

characters on persons they have met or heard about, but it is doubtful whether any one of them, at any rate in modern times, has gone so far as to take for his hero a man straight from the world without so much as troubling to change his name. This Conrad did more than once, notably with Almayer and Captain Beard of the *Judea*.

"Youth" is one of the extreme examples, and, like "The Shadow Line," is a strict autobiographical transcript. It is the same with "The Arrow of Gold." But there is no important or successful story in the whole of Conrad which has not, woven into it, much of the actual stuff of life. Even that is putting it too mildly. There can be few novels by anybody which do not contain a scene, a character, taken from life ; it is the most natural thing in the world to work into your story experiences and episodes which you yourself have lived. But Conrad did more than this ; with him the actual experience becomes the story itself ; it is no longer a convenient incidental : without it the story would not, could not be.

Apart from those fragments of undoctored autobiography which we have already mentioned we have the books (all that remains of Conrad's output, in fact) which present either actual characters in their actual situations, like Falk, or actual characters who in real life did not meet but whom Conrad has brought together for a dramatic clash—that clash itself probably being suggested by some actual situation heard of or experienced in another connection—like "Nostromo" or "Victory." For the rest there are varying permutations of these fixed elements, actual characters and actual situations. "Nostromo," for instance, began with a situation, the theft of a lighter-full of silver on the

South American occidental seaboard, an actual fact, " a vagrant anecdote completely destitute of valuable details." Then, a quarter of a century later, he comes across that anecdote again, this time in a slightly expanded form, part of a sailor's autobiography of which the whole episode took about three pages :

" Nothing to speak of ; but as I looked them over the curious confirmation of the few casual words heard in my early youth evoked the memories of that distant time when everything was so fresh, so surprising, so venturesome, so interesting ; bits of strange coast under the stars, shadows of hills in the sunshine, men's passions in the dusk, gossip half-forgotten, faces grown dim. . . . Perhaps, perhaps, there was still in the world something to write about. Yet I did not see anything at first in the mere story. A rascal steals a large parcel of a valuable commodity—so people say. It's either true or untrue ; and in any case it has no value in itself. To invent a circumstantial account of the robbery did not appeal to me, because my talents not running that way I did not think the game worth the candle. It was only when it dawned on me that the purloiner of the treasure need not necessarily be a con-firmed rogue, that he could be even a man of character, an actor and possibly a victim in the changing scenes of a revolution, it was only then that I had the first vision of a twilight country which was to become the province of Sulaco, with its high shadowy Sierra and its misty Campo for mute witnesses of events flowing from the passions of men short-sighted in good and evil."

It was only then, and then only because in his youth he had once sailed down that coast and now remembered it, because in his childhood he had lived in an unsettled, insurrectory land, because in his youth again he had known and been guided by the very man who in certain circumstances might have carried out that very deed, the stealing of a lighter-full of silver. So the stage is set in a land he had got the flavour of, a political state with which he was familiar, and then peopled with characters he had met and known, Nostromo himself is brought over from the Mediterranean of Conrad's youth. In his own words: " . . . mainly Nostromo is what he is because I received the inspiration for him in my early days from a Mediterranean sailor. Those who have read certain pages of mine will at once see what I mean when I say that Dominic the *padrone* of the *Tremolino* might under given circumstances have been a Nostromo. At any rate Dominic would have understood the younger man perfectly—if a little scornfully. . . . Many of Nostromo's speeches I have heard first in Dominic's voice." And it does not stop at that. Antonia is imported with her grave revolutionary ardour from insurrectory Poland ; Mrs. Gould is plainly a version, the finest version extant, of the same woman who served Conrad as a model for Mrs. Travers and for others . . . one could continue through the whole densely populated gallery, not supplying the names of the people on whom he based his characters, but pointing to the fundamental similarity between this character in " Nostromo " and that character in another book, indicative that both are based on some prototype in the actual world. One could fill pages, a whole volume, with the complete *catalogue raisonné* of episodes, situations and people heard of or directly known to Conrad and later introduced variously into his novels; but this is material for the biographer rather than the critic. It is stressed here only for the sake of our immediate point, that Conrad lacked the faculty of invention.

Time after time one comes across the same incident, the same situation, the same character, sometimes made much of, sometimes referred to fleetingly, manifestly taken from life and rendered with a slightly changing emphasis. And this is one of the secrets of Conrad's incomparable verisimilitude, the motive word for which, as Ford Madox Ford has so suitably emphasized, is "justification." Justification which involves the refusal to take anything for granted; the firm establishment in the reader's credibility of every single character, no matter how subsidiary, of every single episode, no matter how quintessentially incidental. Again, one might fill a volume with examples of Conrad's scrupulousness in this matter of justification, examples sometimes limited to a parenthetical phrase, sometimes expanded to a chapter; but if the game is worth playing at all the reader will most enjoy playing it by himself. A single example of what I mean may be taken from "Falk," and by quoting a certain passage at some length we shall kill two birds with one stone; we shall supply ourselves with an admirable example of this principle of justification and at the same time see how Conrad got every ounce of effect from his life's experience.

"Falk," of course, is primarily and essentially the story of the love affair of that strange creature whose life was blighted by the fact that in wholly gruesome circumstances he had repeatedly dined off human flesh. That is the story. The particular interest is the irresistible power of

the impulse towards self-preservation in this inoffensive
creature. It is told in the first person, and the narrator,
instead of taking the circumstances for granted, begins by
justifying his presence at the heart of the situation, which is
the barque owned by Hermann, the comfortable little
German *Schifführer*. Lest the reader shall wonder how
on earth a busy sea captain found so much time to sit about
in a brother officer's cuddy the circumstances are rapidly
explained down to the final, living, circumstantial detail—
and the reader exclaims (if he is innocent) at Conrad's
amazing fertility of invention . . . to throw away what
is really a story in itself as an incidental paragraph—the
noble prodigality, the Mozartian superabundance !

The narrator of the story, Conrad of course, found
Hermann's hospitality convenient because he had been
having " a rather worrying time on board my own ship.
I had been appointed ex-officio by the British Consul to
take charge of her after a man who had died suddenly,
leaving for the guidance of his successor some suspiciously
unreceipted bills, a few dry-dock estimates hinting at
bribery, and a quantity of vouchers for three years' extravagant expenditure ; all these mixed up together in a dusty old
violin-case lined with ruby velvet. I found besides a large
account-book which, when opened hopefully, turned out
to my infinite consternation to be filled with verses—page
after page of rhymed doggerel of a jovial and improper
character, written in the neatest minute hand I ever did see.
In the same fiddle-case a photograph of my predecessor,
taken lately in Saigon, represented in front of a garden view,
and in company of a female in strange draperies, an elderly,
squat, rugged man of stern aspect in a clumsy suit of black

broadcloth, and with the hair brushed forward above the temples reminding one of boar's tusks. Of a fiddle, however, the only trace on board was the case, its empty husk, as it were ; but of the two last freights the ship had indubitably earned of late, there were not even the husks left. It was impossible to say where all the money had gone to. It wasn't on board. It had not been remitted home ; for a letter from the owners, preserved in a desk evidently by the merest accident, complained mildly enough that they had not been favoured by a scratch of the pen for the last eighteen months. There were next to no stores on board, not an inch of spare rope or a yard of canvas. The ship had been run bare, and I foresaw no end of difficulties before I could get her ready for sea."

And so it goes on for another paragraph or two—all entirely incidental, none of it having any direct bearing on the sad case of Falk, yet all of it helping to build up a palpable environment in which Falk may play out his little act.

But Conrad was not, whatever else he may have been, Mozartian ; he was not superabundant. And this very incident, apparently so beautifully imagined, is, in elaborated form, served up ten years later as the basis of a long story, of " The Shadow Line," declared by Conrad to be pure, unadulterated autobiography. In " The Shadow Line " the defunct captain with the violin-case and the unsuitable passion dominates the greater part of the book, the memory of him driving the mate to the edge of madness, and his gutting the ship of stores all but causing wholesale calamity—for he had also pawned the quinine needed for the salvation of a fever-stricken crew. The mystery of the violin is also solved—the captain had jumped overboard with it. It is interesting to see how Conrad has taken just enough and no more from his actual experience to embellish the story of " Falk." The defunct captain is rendered sharply, but his suicide goes unmentioned ; and the captain's irresponsibility is given as the sole reason for the narrator's delay in the harbour, when in fact the main reason was the raging fever on board. Just enough is taken and no more. Conrad does not twist or adapt his own experience in any way, even for that little paragraph : what he offers is nothing but the truth, but it is not the whole truth.

That is as good an example as any (if by no means a subtle one) both of Conrad's justifying and of his employment of actual experiences in the most unimportant contexts. It is an example which could be paralleled certainly by hundreds of others, and probably by thousands. We discover, in a word, that what seems prodigality of imagination, of invention, is nothing but a capacity for using every fragment of experience so that it tells to the last ounce.

It may be asked why, when Conrad's own life was so packed with significant episodes, he should trouble to invent. . . . There was no need for it, so the fact that he did not proves nothing. There were, however, times when necessity did arise, when Conrad's first-hand experiences dried up. " Nostromo " itself is not in its main lines first-hand experience (although it is packed with minor transcripts from life). In the preface to that book Conrad himself has written that he was caused " some concern " by the fact that " after finishing the last story of the *Typhoon* volume it seemed somehow that there was nothing more in the world to write about. This strangely negative but disturbing mood lasted some little time ; and then, as with many of my longer stories, the first hint for *Nostromo* came to me in the shape of a vagrant anecdote completely destitute of valuable details."

And it is a fact that the " Typhoon " volume marks the end of the period in which Conrad drew almost invariably from his most vivid *personal* experiences. Things known were more or less exhausted ; there was " nothing more in the world to write about." " The Shadow Line " and " The Arrow of Gold " come much later, it is true, but we also know that there was for Conrad in the two major experiences enshrined in those books something almost sacrosanct. Of Rita de Lastaola probably he never intended to write at all, and the wonder is that he was ready to before he died. Quite apart from the period of empti-ness preceding " Nostromo," we can gather from the letters that there were many times when there was nothing in the world to write about, and confirmation is provided by the manner in which he leapt at stray hints. " The Secret Agent," for instance, owed its conception to a casual remark by Ford Madox Ford. And at such barren times one gathers that not only did he attempt no fabrication out of the blue, as it were, but that it never seemed even to occur to him to try. He simply waited, more or less resigned, until he heard something which stimulated his imagination. Even in that last unfinished book, " Suspense," in which Conrad seems to have soared beyond so many of his limita-tions, the chief characters are taken directly from life—Adèle, her husband, her parents, Cosmo, and Mr. Latham ; and even the trivial detail of circumstances is retained—

to the extent of Latham being made a Yorkshireman, after his prototype. And in addition to this there is evidence to suggest that the actual episode to do with Elba was taken directly from another source, although, since the episode is hardly begun before the narrative ceases, it is impossible to dogmatize. Conrad was not an inventor. And if we want further proof of this we have his own admissions. He seems to have regarded the inventive faculty not only as unnecessary but even as pernicious in a novelist. We find in his prefaces and essays a number of semi-humorous references to the " lies " of novelists, and on one or two occasions he is plainly serious, as in the following from the preface to " Heart of Darkness " :

" As for the story itself, it is true enough in its essentials. The sustained invention of a really telling lie demands a talent which I do not possess."

He has just informed the reader that " Youth " may be taken as a strict transcription of experience, whereas, almost apologetically, " Heart of Darkness " is less strict :

" It is experience pushed a little (and only a very little) beyond the actual facts of the case for the perfectly legiti-mate, I believe, purpose of bringing it home to the minds and bosoms of the readers. There it was no longer [as in ' Youth '] a matter of sincere colouring. It was like another art altogether. That sombre theme had to be given a sinister resonance, a tonality of its own, a continued vibration that, I hoped, would hang in the air, and dwell on the ear after the last note had been struck."

The deficiency of Conrad's inventive faculty is a definite deficiency like any other, but aided by his other qualities Conrad made a virtue out of necessity. He had his inspired common sense, his sharp insight into motives, his astounding power of observation, and his incandescent vision ; and unable to make up things in his own head he trained his battery of qualities on the actual things surrounding him— with what results ! And if his invention was weak his sympathetic imagination had no limits ; before it could begin to function it required a spring-board of actual fact, but when such a fact was provided, " lingering with half-open wings like those birds that cannot rise easily from a flat level, it found a pinnacle from which to soar up into the skies."

So much for the fact, but, interesting as it is, the true importance of it lies in the implications. In our normally casual manner of thinking we should, I think, declare unhesitatingly that among the first qualities required in a successful novelist is just this quality of invention. Yet here we have a man, manifestly great and undeniably successful, demonstrably lacking in it. This is the kind of complication which makes it necessary to leave off contemplating the particular and turn for a moment to generalities, to first principles ; in this instance to make a few guesses at what the novel, as an art form, may really be said to amount to.

Every work of art may be regarded as a mirror of the artist's consciousness in face of a given stimulus. That is a definition not of art but of a single aspect of it. The universal stimulus is life itself, human life in relation to the universe as a whole. That is to say, the highest common factor of all the arts is the expression of perception in terms of the medium employed. An expression of perception is implicitly an expression of emotion, and vice versa. Perception and emotion being indivisible (the one is the immediate and ineluctable stimulus of the other, and the other heightens the sensitiveness of the one), perception being the passive half of a complex state, emotion the active half, the expression of emotion is the expression of perception. The existence of art depends absolutely on the indivisibility of the two, the initial perceiving conditioning the emotion, and in that emotion being implicit the initial perception. The business of the artist is to convey the sum of his perceptions with absolute precision and lucidity. This may be done directly or indirectly, by parable or by simple statement.

In the case of music, which is regarded by many as the most perfect of arts, which Conrad himself called " the art of arts," the composer sets to work by arousing emotion in the hearer's breast which is, as nearly as possible, the duplicate of the emotion aroused in his own breast by his own perception. Ideally, the communication of this emotion immediately and automatically puts all who, through the composer, experience it in possession of the initial perception of which it is the inseparable corollary.

The musician is primarily concerned with the expression of his own emotion in terms of sound. He may be more romantically inclined than classically, in which case he will be content to record each changing mood for its own sake ; or he may be more classically than romantically inclined, in which case he will attempt to harmonize his moods into a balanced confession of faith, a whole which shall be greater than the sum of its parts. In either case the process is essentially the same : the purpose of Bach is in no way different from the purpose of Tschaikowski : the music of each is no more than a record of a state of mind.

Compared with the novelist the musician seems to have an uncomplicated task. For the novelist, while also concerned with the expression of his own emotions, must not only employ words which, for the purposes of this argument, are the equivalent of the musician's tones, but also the activities of other people, *their* emotions, their perceptions, in a word. We find that the novelist, the realistic novelist, is prevented from ever revealing his own personality, the sum of his vision, " neat," as it were ; it is manifest only between the lines, or else mirrored and cross-mirrored by each of the innumerable aspects of even the simplest tale. In a word, while a symphony is a direct statement a novel is a highly complex allegory.

Music is the only art through which emotion can be communicated in the abstract and without parable. And it is this, together with the matter of verbal ambiguity, which makes so many people, including Conrad, regard it as supreme among the arts. It has the " magic suggestiveness " which all else lacks. But this belief that music is the most perfect of the arts (and how widely spread it is may be seen from the contemporary attempts of painters, sculptors, and poets to achieve an abstraction comparable to that of music), although in the first instance it is soundly based on the assumption that it is the primary duty of art to mirror the artist's own soul in relation to the exterior world, has inherent in its tenure a confusion. The confusion is between the means and the end. For a duty is not the same as an end. The primary duty of the sentries out-

100

side Buckingham Palace appears to the innocent to consist of standing rigidly to attention, stamping from time to time vehemently up and down, and (I take it) challenging suspicious strangers. The end, however, is the bodily safety of the Royal Family and all that appertains thereto. The end of art is illumination.

The faculty uniquely possessed by music of conveying abstract emotion (the term " abstract " here is a little rough and ready and requires looking into ; but it will do for this kind of generalization) is also its only faculty. If the communication of absolute emotion were the only end of art music would plainly be supreme, so infinitely superior to all the other arts as to render them negligible, a position just as plainly intolerable. But there are two things which upset this supremacy. In the first place the emotion is not the end but the means. It is the sequel to the composer's individual perception, from which it is inseparable, and it is communicated to his hearers so that they may share his perception, which it reflects. It is, in short, a roundabout method of procedure. The painter and the novelist, the realistic novelist, are not required to communicate emotion as such simply because they are in the position, their skill being equal to their task, to render their original perceptions. In the second place, and more importantly, although music deals in abstract emotion that very virtue is a limitation, since all that can be communicated is the composer's emotion in face of the world as a whole and never, except on a very limited ground, in face of specific phenomena. Composers themselves have been troubled by this, and to overcome the difficulty we have the conception of the genre known as programme music, beginning several

centuries back (so far as modern European music is concerned) with the naïve attempts of Kuhnau to translate the
struggle between David and Goliath into terms of the
harpsichord, continuing through Mendelssohn right down
to the Richard Strauss of " Don Quixote "—and later still,
of course, in watered numbers. Yet in every case where
the composer attempts any detailed rendering there is a
sense of strain. Programme music, so called, is wholly
successful only when, as in Mendelssohn's " Fingal's Cave "
Overture or in Smetana's " Moldavia " or Sibelius's
" Tapiola," the composer has contented himself with
generalizing his impressions and evoking the enveloping
atmosphere, as apprehended by him, of his subject. The
Mendelssohn Overture does give us a rocky and serrated
coast most vividly, but it might be any coast, any cave,
outside the tropic zone. There is nothing specific. And
this, fundamentally, does not differ in kind from the
music commonly called absolute, such as a Mozart
Symphony, since this mirrors the state of a composer's
soul in face of his environment just as the Mendelssohn
Overture mirrors its composer's soul in face of a rocky
coast.

For rendering a generalized state of mind music remains
the supreme art and will probably continue so for ever,
although there are signs that prose fiction has latent in it a
good deal more of that " magic suggestiveness " than has
yet appeared on the surface. The artist, however, with
illumination as his end, is concerned not merely with
lighting up the universe as a whole, but also its countless
tiny facets. An art which can generalize as music general-
izes as well as particularize as painting and the novel do

would be most triumphantly " the art of arts," but as it is the various branches seem more or less complementary. Conrad's homage to music is understandable, how understandable I hope we shall see later on ; but regarded now simply from our immediate point of view it is surely no more than the cry of an artist desiring to sum up his generalized impressions of the universe in a single moment of incandescent intensity. It is the intensity of expression attainable in music which is, indeed, its lure ; the freedom to express an infinitely complex state of mind in a few moments of time. The novelist must proceed more slowly.

But in the end he too will arrive. For although his task is to render the multitudinous phenomena of the world, the cumulative effect of all this detail will surely provide the attentive reader with, as a strong and ever-sounding overtone, his perceptions of the universe as a whole. A musician can do this more directly than a novelist or a painter, but, it seems to me, no more effectively in the long run. He can do this, but in no circumstances can he deploy into the specific. And frequently, as the composers of programme music bear witness, the need to do this is intolerably strong. In short, neither the musician nor the novelist nor any other kind of artist can express directly all that a man in his lifetime desires to express ; but indirectly and with the aid of overtones audible only to the most delicate ear, everything may be said. From a novelist's particularizations it is possible to deduce his generalizations, and from a musician's generalizations, if one cares to, one can get a fair enough idea of his perceptions of particular things.

Perhaps we may now agree that the inability of the novelist, the realistic novelist, to present the world with emotion in the abstract is not, above all, a limitation, but a privilege ; a privilege, it is true, like so many privileges, involving hardship. His task is difficult, but if he succeeds his voice is no less clear than the voice of Schubert. He succeeds very seldom. The musician must work directly for the broad effect, the realistic novelist for the detail ; and there is nobody who can say that the one is more blessed than the other.

The raw material of the novelist is everything that can be rendered in prose, rendered, not reported. There is a great difference. A landscape reported is a sober inventory of natural objects called by their names, and the use of imagery must be confined to images that have become common currency and will give no shock to the reader. But a landscape rendered is the description of the writer's own individual perception of that landscape. It is the difference between Frith and Sickert. Also, and very important it is, things can be rendered which cannot possibly be reported—those subjective impressions betrayed by the peculiar choice of words which convey the enveloping atmosphere of a scene, the colour of the scene as the novelist apprehends it. A passable definition of rendering might be the objective reporting of one's subjective impressions.

It is possible for the writer to find subjects the rendering of which will allow him to be very high-falutin' in the exposure of his own soul, but the realistic novelist is denied such extravagance. Dealing mainly with the activities of men and women, his first problem, if he hopes to carry any conviction, is to keep them true to life. This is an admirable discipline. It obviates undue self-consciousness and self-dramatization, which is the bane of all art. For the novelist, if he is scrupulous and if he deals in that kind of novel which must have both feet firmly planted in actuality, is of necessity so preoccupied with keeping his characters and his situations *actual* that he has little time left for reflecting on the sublime miracle of his own soul. That is left to take care of itself, which it does if it is worth anything at all. The realistic novelist finds himself forced to attend to reality as it appears to him while never forgetting how it appears to others, and the quality of his perception may be determined by the individual reader. The one criterion is whether or not he appears to penetrate to the inner truth of the situation under treatment, or, more accurately, to one or several of the innumerable aspects of this truth.

That applies only to the realistic novel. The use of this kind of term is horribly ambiguous, and it is not entirely the fault of the present writer. To express one's meaning one has either to invent new terms and risk a charge of arrogance or else attempt to make clear the precise sense in which the conventional terms are, for the immediate matter in hand, to be understood. The term " realistic " applied to the novel is especially tricky in this respect. It is used here to include the bulk of all great novels, all those in fact which depend for their effect on a fidelity to the external appearance of life as it is lived. To justify himself as an artist the realistic novelist must reveal at least one aspect of the inner truth of a given situation without obtrusively distorting the rigid, unambiguous shell of outer truth, " the actualities which are the daily bread of the public mind," to use Conrad's own words in meditation on the outer truth of the wretched swindler, de Barral. For the purposes of this study the realistic novel is opposed to the fantasy, which may or may not be fantastic. The opposition is perfect, for while the realistic novelist is concerned with the direct communication of his own perceptions of specific objects, these perceptions arousing in the reader's breast the appropriate emotions, a fantasy is fundamentally a fable invented for the communication of the author's generalized perceptions of life as a whole, and, like music, concerned more with the communication of the emotion governed by the perceptions than with the perceptions themselves, a fable which may or may not have reference to actuality.

It should be clear by now, I think, that realism in our sense has nothing to do with the faithful reporting of reality or actuality, but with the rendering, in terms of the novelist's personal vision (which, of course, is for him ineluctable) of life. It may be countered that this is done by everybody, that " The Way of an Eagle " expresses Miss E. M. Dell's personal vision of life as accurately as " Chance " expresses Conrad's. But everybody does not : the popular lady and gentleman novelists, the spinners of excitingly romantic yarns who make no pretence to art, pretend no more to base their romances on actuality. They deal with invented people in invented circumstances, and their works, strictly speaking, belong to a class of fantasy ; happily, very happily, to determine the precise dividing line between the various types of fantasy developed by Miss Berta Ruck, by Miss Virginia Woolf, by Mr. John Collier, by Miss Rose Macaulay, and by Mr. Ronald Fraser is indubitably beyond the scope of our present study.

Plainly the two categories are each of an extremely com-
pendious nature.

If fantasy depends on fluent invention, nothing so far in
this little inquiry has suggested that the realistic novel needs
it in the least.   If the novelist's (and henceforth we shall be
concerned solely with the realistic novelist, as all too
broadly defined) primary care is to illuminate, there is only
one thing which he can illuminate, and that is life ; and
since he cannot illuminate the whole of life (for even
Tolstoi, as George Moore has mentioned, omitted to work
into " War and Peace " a description of a yacht race) he
must take particular and typical affairs in an attempt to
show their universal significance.   And if this is all he can
do, and it is, and if the light of his perception reflected from
a particular affair can suffuse the universe itself with light
(which, when a great novelist is at work, is done), illuminating generally the heart of mankind, where does invention
come in ?   The raw material is the affair, an affair which
to the everyday, apathetic eye may seem commonplace or
may seem spectacular, but of which the actualities are the
only things that strike home.   And when so many affairs
are lying about the world, when indeed a significant affair
is being pursued at every street corner, it seems, it may be
argued, somewhat perverse and unnecessary to invent
additional ones.   It is as though the painter were to invent
a landscape or a model instead of painting from life.   The
capacity to invent in this way is a faculty like any other, and
the man who has it plainly has something that the others
haven't got ; but has it, strictly speaking, anything to do

with the realistic novel? Further, the argument might run, the realistic novelist who invents his characters and situations is complicating his task to quite an unnecessary extent. Such invention, when ready-made situations are lying to hand, is superfluous. It is, moreover, with the best will in the world, liable to lead away from truth. It is not enough for the novelist to describe the actual reality before his eyes; his imagination must be incessantly at work in his effort to get at the inner truth, and in the process of selection and subtle emphasis, with the end of making the rendered actualities of the affair yield up their harvest and reflect the secret inner truth, he may very easily run off the rails, may distort too freely and lose verisimilitude and with it all illusion. This can happen all too easily when he is drawing from life, from a model, the rigid terms of which are a constant to act as a check on an untoward distortion of the actualities. And if there is no model, if the only model existing at all is an invented one dwelling on air in the author's imagination (and how treacherously blurred and wavy are the outlines of the most vividly imagined figure, apparently so square and robust, so clear in many details, yet infinitely elusive when it comes to the co-ordination of every detail in a vital whole—like a figure seen in a dream), how much greater is the danger of the flight from reality?

And, further still, if art is illumination, if the novel, the realistic novel, is concerned with penetrating far below the surface of actuality, if this is true, which it is, what conceivable concern has the novelist, the realistic novelist, with invented characters and situations? How can truth be discovered by illuminating lies?

That is a very possible train of thought, and it seems certain that something like it must have passed through Conrad's mind when he wrote somewhat stand-offishly of the lies of novelists. That it did, or something like it, is confirmed too by his repeated reference to Truth in a sense far narrower than is generally understood when art is in question. For Conrad on several occasions, speaking of the novelist's duty by truth, was quite plainly meaning exterior truth, as, for instance, when he writes in " Under Western Eyes " of " my primary conviction that truth alone is the justification of any fiction which makes the least claim to the quality of art." From the context it is plain that by truth Conrad meant fidelity to the exterior aspects of the affair under treatment.

This argument which we have somewhat impertinently attributed to Conrad—I really do not see on what other grounds he could have based his contempt for invention—has a plausible ring about it, but it is nevertheless a begging of the question. It derives from the assumption that invention is a cerebral trick governed by no laws of inevitability, and that is due, I imagine, to the fact that Conrad's own inability to invent carried quite naturally with it an incomprehension of the true nature of invention. Any quality of which one lacks a vestige will appear in another a somewhat monstrous and unnatural trick. The tendency is to see it as a self-contained attribute existing in a vacuum. And the ability to invent may well have seemed to Conrad as irrelevant, as unconnected with all reasonable faculties, as fortuitous a *trick* as the ability to master the differential calculus may seem to the unmathematical mind—say, the present writer's.   I am not so sure of the differential calculus, but the quality of invention is not an irrelevant, unnatural accomplishment having no reference to man's higher nature.

If we accept as truth that nothing is new under the sun, invention is seen plainly as a process of association, the association of already existing elements, or their analysis and reassociation.   And that, indeed, whether we accept the platitude or not, is what all invention comes to, the invention of the novelist as well as that of the engineer.   It is a particular kind of synthesis, original synthesis.

But in the novel there are various kinds of synthesis, and these may broadly speaking be bundled into two separate categories.   First there is the synthesis of qualities into living characters and of motives into situations ; secondly there is the synthesis of characters and situations into plots. The first I should like to call psychological synthesis, the second formal synthesis ; and it is the first, the quality of psychological synthesis or invention, which Conrad lacked; the quality of formal invention he had most highly developed, as we shall be seeing later on : but this, as a rule, is not what is meant by invention in a novelist.

The elements combined in this psychological synthesis may be as minute and multitudinous as the cells of the human body.   Anybody can pick up an armful of bolts, nuts, rods, tubing, cog-wheels, and plating and contrive somehow to fasten them together, if only with a piece of string ; but the result is by no means invariably a machine. And similarly anybody can take a handful of complexes, features, characteristics, and the rest and label them John

Smith ; but the result is not always a character. The only criterion of the machine is its workability and of the character its convincingness. And these handfuls of elements can only be assembled to make a workable machine or a convincing character by a man who has a complete and intimate understanding of the component parts, each for what it is, a full comprehension of the laws governing their individual functions, together with a clear and steadfast vision of the particular functions of the machine desired and the particular effect of the character desired. Several processes are here involved, the most important being the capacity to visualize clearly something which the physical eye has never seen.

The invention of the novelist, the serious realistic novelist, is a complicated and logical process made in two stages. All the material he has to work with is already embodied in the men and women inhabiting this planet. A characteristic or a complex is neither until it is embodied in a human being ; and this means that to find his raw material the inventing novelist must take isolated elements from a variety of different characters. The first stage, then, is one of analysis, the disassociation of the innumerable elements contributing to the character of a ready-made human being. A thousand characters analysed, the novelist has a large pile of qualities which he is free to combine again, to reassociate into new patterns, into new human beings. But obviously this can be no arbitrary process. There are laws governing the functioning of the various elements, and these laws must be understood so that the right elements may be combined to give a required effect, just as the qualities of the primary colours must be understood by the painter before he can get his desired effects. This kind of knowledge is essentially empirical. The analysis having been made, the isolated elements being understood, the stage is now set for reassociation.

What I have indicated here as a highly conscious and laborious process is, of course, in practice a semi-conscious and instantaneous one. The solution is based on what is known as intuition. But intuition itself is based on hidden mental processes continuing incessantly over a lifetime ; and these processes, simplified to excess and rationalized, must be something like the one I have tried to indicate. The only purpose in indicating it is to show that invention in the novel or in any other sphere is not an arbitrary process of making up out of the blue.

The reassociation is a simpler matter, in practice at any rate. In theory it should be possible to take an assortment of qualities, combine them scientifically and be surprised at the result. In practice the novelist is generally working for a definite end, and the reassociation is conditioned by his needs. Because of this it would be senseless to pursue the theory of the matter any further. All we are concerned with is what in practice happens. Why should a novelist, a realistic novelist, invent at all ? That an invented character or situation is not necessarily a lie we have seen, and that an invented account of the theft of a lighter-full of silver by an imaginary rascal need not necessarily be, as Conrad would have it, " a circumstantial account of a robbery," but the narrative of an inevitable action— granted the just composition of the rascal's character in the first instance. But there still remains the argument, plausible enough, that such invention is superfluous, that

with so many ready-made affairs and characters lying to
hand the energy expended on invention could be better
employed in other directions. That is an argument,
however, which holds good only if the novelist is omniscient, if, in a word, he is God. Doubtless scattered through
time and space there have been characters and situations
involving every conceivable combination and permutation
of elements and motives. The omnipresent, omniscient
novelist would merely have to seize on those characters
and those affairs which interested him most, which seemed
to him best suited to his particular gifts of revelation and
understanding. The novelist, however, say Conrad or
Henry James, is neither omniscient, omnipresent, nor
omnipotent. His mind runs on certain lines, not on all
lines ; certain characters and situations appeal to him,
stimulate his imagination, and seem to him highly significant. By treating of them he communicates his sense of
their significance to a wider public. But in a world covering so many million square miles and populated by so many
million inhabitants, our novelist has a fairly small chance of
finding among the few thousand people and situations he
comes across in his lifetime any of the, for him, perfect
permutations of character and situation. They are suggested to him by approximations in others. He may have
seen or heard of a certain man who stimulates his imagination. He decides to write about that man and finds that
for æsthetic purposes his nature would best be revealed by a
particular kind of clash with another character of a particular kind. The model of the other character may not
lie ready to hand, so he is forced to invent, to combine the
required qualities into a vital whole ; he will, the chances

113

are, find that these required qualities invariably go with other qualities which may have a cancelling effect. He then has three ways open to him. He may jettison the character and try again, or he may use the character in quite a different situation arising inevitably out of that character, or, intent on his main situation, he may suppress the complementary qualities and work with an unnatural abortion. This is the danger of working from the situation to the character, and many novelists have come to grief over it. I instance Henry James in " The Wings of the Dove." More easy and more generally successful is the visualizing of a certain type which interests you and which you know will behave approximately on certain lines, the invention of detail to turn the type into a unique individual whom you will then lead into the particular kind of situation you had in mind, bringing in other characters and episodes either taken direct from life or invented.

Or again, and more commonly still, I imagine, the novelist is struck by a person he sees, is struck and actively interested to the point of thinking earnestly about him in an attempt to fathom the depths of his personality. That much accomplished by intuition based on a wide experience of men and women, by analysis, the problem arises, if the subject is still interesting enough, how to convey his conclusions, his understanding, to the public at large. . . . Here we have Mr. Brown celebrated among his acquaintances chiefly for his reserve and the juxtaposition of frayed trousers and immaculate spats. His general state of mind is plain ; there is nothing about him that our novelist does not know except—the facts ; and yet it is by displaying the facts and the facts alone that he, as the slave of actuality and not of fantasy, can make his perception clearer. The facts will have to be invented, and that should not be a very difficult matter. The novelist knows approximately, probably pretty exactly, the man's state of mind, and it is obvious enough what he was, say, twenty years ago. Men of his type may get into the state in which we now find him through a variety of causes. There are several things which may have contributed to his present state. And these he considers. He finds that a certain combination of causes would have led irresistibly to that present state, very possibly several combinations of circumstances and violent contacts with a variety of characters. All that remains is selection with an eye to dramatic interest or to subtlety, or to the shape of a story. And there he has the rudiments of his plot, the facts of the matter (unquestionable facts if the novelist is any good at his job), and there you have your invention. This kind of method is probably the one most widely practised of all, and therefore most abused. It is the method Arnold Bennett must have used in " The Old Wives' Tale " ; its variants are legion.

For invention in a realistic novel is not a self-contained talent existing in a vacuum ; it is the provision of facts to explain a certain state ; in worthy hands it is an inevitable, an almost scientific process. It is the most valuable of all qualities to writers less fortunate than Conrad in their travels.

We know from Conrad's work that he did not invent, and from his own declarations that he regarded invention as suspect. Yet we also know that he had the power of analysis highly developed, and analysis we have seen to be the first of the two stages of invention. Conrad, then, would have known as much about Mr. Brown as our imaginary novelist, but he could not have put him into revealing action. He would have remained at a loss opposite the passive Mr. Brown if that gentleman had been the only character left to treat in the world. He could have written a detailed and shrewd analysis of his character in the form of an essay, a sketch, but he could not have thrown him into self-revealing action, which is the novelist's task. He could have sat in a railway carriage face to face with that interesting and significant specimen for all eternity, staring at him not blankly but with troubled irritation. For ever—unless . . . unless Mr. Brown suddenly leapt from passivity into activity, committing a dramatic action which would instantly strike his pondering *vis-à-vis* as highly illuminating, such as leaping from the carriage window with a muttered curse for a woman's name . . . or, unless in the course of whiling away eternity with reserved conversation Mr. Brown were to hint (a hint would have been enough) at some characteristic action of his past, characteristic and dramatic. And then the hunt would begin in earnest. No longer at fault Conrad would fasten on to that action, describe it, worry it, delve into it, examine it in every conceivable aspect, in all its implications, write up everything he found to say about it and use it as a central affair of a book—no, not the central affair, the very stuff and matter of the book. And when it was all over, when Conrad had rendered this action, this affair, to his own all but insatiable satisfaction— well, there you would have a first-class portrait of Mr.

Brown down to the last button, sprung from that incident like a ramified oak from an acorn. The portrait is the result of imagination, not of invention. And imagination is a subjective process, invention an objective one.

That, in its crudest form, is the Conradian method. It begins either with an action like the theft of the lighter-full of silver, which is suddenly connected with a familiar character, or it begins with a given character engaged in characteristic action. Conrad was perfectly capable of understanding a character subjectively. He could say of him—he seems to me to run on such and such lines, and ten to one he would be right ; but because of some cerebral obstruction he was unable to carry his discovery to its logical conclusion and say, characters of such and such a nature generally behave in a certain way ; and behaviour of this kind generally leads to such and such a situation. It is the task of the psychologist to investigate this hiatus for its own sake. We are concerned only with its effect on the novels. And for us it is enough to say that whatever the cause of it, it seems to imply a constitutional incapacity to visualize objectively any phenomena of any kind which is not presented to him through one or other of his senses. That means that he could not combine motives into a situation or complexes and characteristics, of which he was perfectly aware, into a character—simply because he could not visualize the complete effect and consequently had nothing to work towards.

But of infinitely more importance to us—and here the circle closes—being unable to form an objective image of anything not presented to his senses (including, then, the supersensuous), he was barred from visualizing objectively

117

the train of thought proceeding in the mind of another man. He was aware intellectually of the other man's state of mind, just as he could be aware intellectually of concrete phenomena unseen by him, but he was unable to transform an intellectual concept into a sensuous image, to dramatize a state of mind. He could not invent. He could not see things which were not, or which never had been, before his eyes. His whole magnificent perceptiveness depended absolutely on the senses. The anecdote in the sailor's autobiography called to mind scenes witnessed in his youth on that very coast, and these called other scenes to mind, scenes with Dominic on the Mediterranean—all sensuous images. On that foundation, to transfer Dominic from Marseilles to the occidental seaboard was an easy matter. He can look into the depths of another man's mind. His astounding power of physical vision enables him to tell a character from its exterior manifestations. He is, I imagine, supremely instinctive. We catch the scent of a rose and say to ourselves, that is a rose's scent, there must be a rose near. We are aware first of the scent, then of the proximity of a flower. A dog catches the smell of a rabbit and there is no conscious association ; the smell *is* the rabbit. And similarly Conrad sees a droop of an eyelid which to most of us would suggest a certain trait in the character's make-up ; but for Conrad that drooping eyelid *is* the trait. He has received an impression. To objectify the physical basis of that impression he has only to describe the eyelid's droop, to draw from the model ; and this he can do to perfection because of his extraordinary power over words. But to objectify the psychological con-clusions of that impression he is forced to analyse, an intellectual process, and then to recreate, to transform the elements revealed by his analysis into a sensuous image, a train of thought on the part of the character—this involving the ability to visualize something in itself invisible to the senses and to translate it into terms of sensuous apprehension.

And thus we come round again to the beginning of our inquiry, to Conrad's avoidance of the interior monologue or anything like it, to the failure of " The Return " and to the success of the indirect narrative, to Marlow who is " a bit of a bore." And Marlow we find indeed a creature of necessity. For it was he among other aids who enabled Conrad to illuminate with subjective comment states of mind which he could never have rendered objectively because he could not invent, because he could not visualize what he had never seen. We find that at the back of his strange psychological limitations is precisely this incapacity to invent ; we find that he was an analytical psychologist of a most distinguished order, but not a creative psychologist at all. But that is very far from saying that he was not a creative artist.

VI

W E have by now, I hope, some idea of the extraordinary circumstances governing Conrad's art. His use of the indirect narrative with the aid of Marlow and other devices we are familiar with. On the assumption that there is nothing causeless, if not under the sun then at least in the expression of a responsible mind, we have looked for the reason for Conrad's choice of method and found it to lie in the attempt of an entirely subjective temperament to live up to a self-imposed ideal of objectivity. If Marlow is a bore, which anyone is at liberty to think, Conrad is also a bore ; the two are inseparable.

I have already quoted Mr. Garnett's phrase, to be found in his preface to " Letters from Joseph Conrad," that Marlow came into being simply because he saved Conrad trouble. That is a curious thing to say about a scrupulous artist with an extremely high opinion of his medium ; in a sense, nevertheless, it is true, but not in the sense, I imagine, that Mr. Garnett intended. If it can be said that an Englishman speaks English because it saves him trouble, then the phrase about Marlow is true ; if it can be said that a man walks on the towpath rather than swims to his destination to save himself trouble, then it is true. But we do not as a rule walk rather than swim to save ourselves trouble, but because it is our natural means of progression. To save ourselves trouble we ride rather than walk, and Conrad never, never rode.

The phrase might possibly be true in another sense, although here we are getting on to dangerous ground. Marlow was not the only device used by Conrad to give a subjective eye an objective focus. In " Nostromo " he took up a standpoint exceedingly difficult to maintain, the standpoint of the objective observer recording physically observed facts with such accuracy that they reveal their inner significance to the reader. The standpoint is not maintained with perfect consistency throughout the book ; at times a junior Marlow is successfully introduced in the person of Decoud, and at times a train of thought is rendered or a passage of interior monologue, usually with not the happiest effect ; but the main attitude is the recording and selection of observed facts. In " The Secret Agent " we have an all but perfect *tour de force* in another technique which we shall have to glance at later on. And then we have the first person stories. It may be true to say that Conrad found all these methods more trying than the Marlow method, even that method as employed in " Chance," and he may have taken Marlow as the lesser of two evils. But to jump out of the fire and into the frying-pan is a gesture surely inadequately described as a saving of trouble.

The only book in which the Marlow device is the obvious device is " Youth," but if Marlow is the line of least resistance here, for once the line of least resistance is the right line. " Youth " is a personal experience of Conrad's which he desired to present neat and untampered with, to

121

relate at first hand ; the subject is less a set of facts than a subjective mood haloing a set of facts. And this cannot possibly be done by an external rendering ; there must on the part of the hero be a great deal of thought and feeling in it. To Conrad, unable to render thought and feeling in sustained detail objectively, the employment of the first person is imperative. He could have told the tale himself, as he did in " The Shadow Line," but happily he did not and consequently gained in clarity and vividness. In " Lord Jim " and in " Heart of Darkness " Marlow may have saved him a certain amount of trouble, but he must have caused him a great deal more worry than he saved. And in " Chance " and " Under Western Eyes " the trouble he gives is stupendous. In " Under Western Eyes," indeed, the obstacles raised by that inoffensive teacher of languages are never fully overcome.

Only in these very limited senses, and then all too dangerously, can it be said that Marlow saved Conrad trouble. The idea in any case is a misleading one, for it carries the implication that if he had gone to sufficient trouble he could have written " Chance " in the manner of, say, Ford Madox Ford's Tietjens novels. And this manner was to him an impossibility for the reasons I have tried to suggest.

In perfect opposition to the more usual view of Marlow and all he stands for we have Henry James prostrating himself in a kind of embarrassed, slightly reproachful awe before the technique of " Chance." His reproach, the reproach of a fellow novelist unlikely himself to be accused of ca' canny, is not that Conrad went about saving himself trouble, but that he simply cried out for it and welcomed it wide-armed, or even that he rushed straight into it, open-eyed, and with a self-immolatory ardour almost indecent :

" It places Mr. Conrad absolutely alone as a votary of the way to do a thing that shall make it undergo most doing. The way to do it that shall make it undergo least is the line on which we are mostly used to see prizes carried off ; so that the author of ' Chance ' gathers up on this showing all sorts of comparative distinction. He gathers up at least two sorts—that of bravery in absolutely reversing the process most accredited, and that, quite separate, we make out, of performing the manœuvre under salvos of recognition . . . the general effect of ' Chance ' is arrived at by a pursuance of means to the end in view contrasted w˙·h which every other current form of the chase can only affect us as cheap and futile ; the carriage of the burden or amount of service required on these lines exceeding surely all other such displayed degrees of energy put together."

But while Mr. James, as he would have to (I quote from the essay on " The New Novel "—1914—in " Notes on Novelists "), fully and most delicately recognizes the extreme sublety of the method of " Chance," and while his estimate of Marlow is a thousand times nearer the mark than the usual one, we shall, if we agree on our conclusions as to Conrad's particular psychological limitations, be compelled to dissent, sharply enough, but not at all bluntly, from the implications in that essay that Conrad deliberately went out of his way to make his task as hard as possible. Methods are conditioned by temperament, and the methods Conrad used, or something like them, were the outcome of necessity. It would be more accurate, I think, to say that with the ideal of objectivity before him and ridden by an artist's conscience he had no option but to write " Chance " as he did. The gratuitous element is the ideal of objectivity, which Henry James would have been the first to uphold.

Curiously enough, indeed, in that same article James touches on this matter of objectivity in a way most illuminating for our purpose : " ' Chance ' *is* an example of objectivity, most precious of aims, not only menaced but definitely compromised ; whereby we are in presence of something really of the strangest, a general and diffused lapse of authenticity which an inordinate number of common readers . . . have not only condoned but have emphatically commended. They can have done this but through the bribe of some authenticity other in kind, no doubt, and seeming to them equally great if not greater, which gives back by the left hand what the right hand has, with however dissimulated a grace, taken away. What Mr. Conrad's left hand gives back then is simply Mr. Conrad himself."

Henry James in those passages is concerned chiefly with the difficulty of succeeding with the method of " Chance " once it is fairly under way, a method " ridden . . . by such a danger of steeping his matter in perfect eventual obscuration as we recall no other artist's consenting to with an equal grace." But the first difficulties, and difficulties in themselves of a kind which make the notion of Conrad employing Marlow to save trouble look silly, arise prolifically on the plane of pure mechanics, in the setting of the method in motion.

In " Youth " Marlow is the central figure and the book is about his experience, or his reception of that experience. But " Chance " is not about Marlow at all. It is about everybody but Marlow, indeed ; and this fact is the motive of the first problem of all. Conrad desiring to write about Flora de Barral and Captain Antony, wanting in his way to unveil his characters completely, yet denied by temperament the direct approach, having to deal in shades of apprehension and perception too delicate and fine to be caught by the straightforward treatment of " Nostromo," needed in the story a character to talk round it. The qualifications required of such a commentator are neither common nor few. He must *know*, he must be experienced in life, he must perceive, he must understand, he must be sympathetic, and he must be interested in people for their own sakes. The actors in the story, the protagonists that matter, we know : Mr. and Mrs. Fyne, Roderick Antony and Flora de Barral, the wicked governess, Mr. Powell, Mr. Franklin —not, if one may say so, a very subtle crowd, not one of them sufficiently perceptive and dispassionate to watch a subtly complex situation and interpret it in its finest, most ambiguous shades. And so somebody has to be brought in from the outside, and the obvious man for the job is Marlow, retired from action for the past ten years. Marlow, once he is in, will save Conrad a lot of trouble ; oh, indubitably. . . . But how to get him in ? And one of the most remarkable things about " Chance " and about Conrad's technical brilliance generally, is the satisfactory way in which this excessively thorny problem is solved.

To the casual glance it may seem to add pages to the length of the book, wanton pages : Marlow has not only to be got in, he has also to be held in so that he does not fall out again. Those pages are certainly so much cover for that situation, precarious, yet never allowed to appear so, being held secure by Conrad's infinitely scrupulous justification of Marlow's every action. But they serve other purposes as well ; they must serve other purposes or there can be no valid excuse for their inclusion. With any writer but Conrad there would be no valid excuse.

The thing is managed perfectly. Marlow, who has no business at all in that gallery, is made to have a business. The very first step is hard enough, the initial establishment of his relations with the Fynes. These are not the kind of people one would expect to find in Marlow's circle, and nobody was more aware of that than Conrad. It has to be made clear, Marlow himself makes it clear, that the Fynes are not his friends at all but the merest accidental holiday acquaintances, in a measure amusing to this student of humanity, but even more boring than amusing. So far so good. That in itself is enough to show off the Fynes and even to get Marlow introduced to, or rather into touch with, the mysterious and suicidal " girl-friend," with Miss Smith, Flora de Barral But it is now essential for Marlow to know all about Flora's history up to the all but fatal walk beside the quarry ; and the only way, the only reasonable way, in which he can come upon this is through one or other of the Fynes. This argues a state of intimacy with that family which Marlow did not enjoy and in normal circumstances was never likely to enjoy. And it is here that the average novelist, granted that he had survived even thus far (which is improbable), would almost certainly have run his story on the rocks. He would have committed an

assault on the integrity of character either on the part of
Marlow or of the Fynes by making them all become close
friends. But Conrad, knowing Marlow, knowing the
Fynes, knew perfectly well that such a consummation could
not be hoped for on this side of the grave. It could have
been contrived with some plausibility; he could have
cooked, so to speak, his characters as politicians cook
statistics; he could, out of his infinite resource, easily have
thrown dust into the reader's eyes. But Conrad was never
a thrower of dust, and with extreme ingenuity (whether
conscious or unconscious has no relevance) he contrived to
put Marlow into Mrs. Fyne's confidence while keeping the
two for all normal purposes as far removed from one
another as they ever were, as they for ever must be. This
is achieved with such a show of spontaneity and ease that
one cannot tell whether a certain turn in the story arose out
of that necessity or whether the necessity was miraculously
eased by a certain turn in the story. We have in fact, as
so often throughout " Chance," that perfect fusion of
content and technique which is the greatest delight that art
can offer. The narrative takes on the aspect of a supercharged engine (if so far-fetched a comparison is allowed)
with all that is implied therein. All things, so to speak,
work together for good in a process which I should like to
call super-augmentation of effect, a process which of all
novelists Conrad wrought to most perfection.

We begin with Marlow as a superficial acquaintance, a
tame chess-player for Fyne. By chance he happens to be
walking by the quarry at the precise moment when Flora
is having her suicidal intentions undermined by the antics
of a ridiculous dog. That same dog introduces him to

Flora herself. The next appreciable step forward is Flora's flight to Captain Antony, or rather, in the first instance, her simple disappearance. Marlow is still in no closer communion with the Fynes, but the chance of his walk by the quarry bears fruit, a second crop indeed, since the first was our introduction to Flora. He remembers her evidently unbalanced state of mind, and this memory throws for him an ominous shadow down into the present. It is because of that walk, and only because of that, and at his suggestion (a suggestion he was made to regret after five minutes' experience of Mr. Fyne's pedestrian faculty), that he joins up with Fyne, turns an aimless search into an extremely pointed one, and, its vainness established, returns with Fyne to his house. And there he encounters Mrs. Fyne, for the first time in her life thrown slightly off her balance, and in the emotional hours of the night at that. For a moment Marlow and the Fynes are on common ground. Without establishing an accord Conrad has accomplished a significant contact, significant enough at least to give perfect plausibility to Mrs. Fyne's coming to him for moral support when, on the reception of Flora's letter, she finds herself, again for the first time in her life, openly at odds with her husband. This little quarrel is of extreme importance too, for besides throwing a light of positively blinding illumination on the Fynes themselves it leaves Mrs. Fyne, an outraged woman, in a state of isolation. She must talk to somebody ; she cannot talk to Fyne : and so she turns to the man in whom she imagines herself to have seen a streak of most unmasculine sagacity and against whom she is thrown in her entirely womanly search for support in face of her inoffensive husband. The contact, the intimate contact, is thus established, with Marlow jibbing away all the time and doing his best, as he would, to break it.   But it is, so far as Mrs. Fyne is concerned (and it is *her* contact, Marlow remaining passive), an entirely emotional contact, and when that particular emotion has blown itself out the relapse into the *status quo* is inevitable and normal.   Marlow never set eyes on her again.   But Mrs. Fyne retained her illusion of his sagacity for just long enough to spill enough beans to keep the story running. And from that contact, so hard to establish and so beautifully contrived, Marlow learns about Flora's girlhood all that is necessary for his story.   And from that contact, too, directly springs Marlow's opportunity to get from Flora's own lips her own story and her version of that all-important walk by the quarry.   During all this time Conrad has been getting Marlow in and at the same time making him work for dear life, like an unsalaried apprentice.

For Flora's own narrative was as difficult to contrive as Mrs. Fyne's.   First the meeting has to be contrived (it is made the direct outcome of the false intimacy of Marlow and the Fynes) and then Flora has to reveal her own past, or those aspects of it which she alone knows.   And this, obviously, can only be done with a comparative stranger as the second party.   People will not reveal themselves to their established friends as Flora revealed herself to Marlow ; but wearied by their burden of secret knowledge they are driven to talk to somebody, and there, miraculously at hand, was the perfect listener, perfect in manner and in position, physical position, that is.   And so it goes on.   It is beautiful.

It may be countered that there is nothing particularly original in this, that all life is strung on a chain of cause and effect, and that all novels, if they are to have any air of inevitability, must also be so contrived. And that is true enough as to kind. What is here significant is the degree, the highly complex contrapuntal pattern that is achieved without a hint of strain. The whole of " Chance," in this way, is a masterpiece of construction of a kind that can only be called fugal. The small example we have taken, which we took primarily to show Conrad's inspired handling of Marlow, his working of a stubborn element into a rigid narrative without any sense of strain (and it is enough, I should say, to show that Marlow, even physically, caused Conrad far more trouble than he saved him), also serves to illuminate the contrapuntal texture of the book. Here I do not refer to the sort of counterpoint practised by Mr. Huxley, the simple interweaving of lives, but to a suggestive, æsthetic counterpoint having no reference to actuality objectively recorded. In all Conrad's work every incident, every character, every sentence almost, is made to do at least double duty, and that is the beauty of the fugue. Nowhere is this faculty of significant compression more finely displayed than in " Chance." That one trivial incident, that accident of Marlow walking by the quarry at the moment when the girl had determined to end her life there, is made to serve half a dozen purposes. It gives Marlow his false intimacy with the Fynes ; it gives him his excuse for being outside the East-end hotel early in the morning ; it gives him sufficient acquaintance with Flora to take advantage of that chance meeting ; it gives Conrad his opportunity to provide the reader with a sharp impression of Flora as a person ; it gives Marlow his opportunity to give you the girl's nature as understood by an

intelligent and perceptive outsider ; it brings into the book
in the most delicate manner imaginable the first hint of the
fatality which is later to increase and pervade it ; it provides the episode of the dog, so perfectly done, which later,
during that street-corner conversation, sends a beam of
illumination flashing down into the present from the past,
assuring for Conrad his ceaselessly sought closeness of
texture and strengthening the ironic mood.

This kind of thing in prose fiction is, with " cutting " in
the cinema, the only thing strictly analogous to musical
counterpoint in all art.   And of all music the contrapuntal is the highest, since it permits of the simultaneous
expression of innumerable shades of meaning.   To its
supremacy Mozart, Schubert, and Beethoven, the world's
three greatest composers besides Bach, bear witness ; in
their maturity they all three resort to the fugue for the
expression of the inexpressible, the fugue with its infinite
power of suggestion.   And the greatness of Conrad as a
novelist may be measured by the success of what amounts
to a contrapuntal structure in his greatest works.

A brief examination of the elementary difficulties brought
on Conrad's head by Marlow in " Chance " has led us
straight into a technical consideration of his work as a whole.
It is not easy here to keep the various elements of technique
neatly pigeon-holed.   The first technical problem of the
novelist is the establishment and preservation of his illusion,
but this problem sooner or later is found to be inseparably
bound up with the wider problem of how he is to get the
last ounce out of his subject.   Marlow himself is a clear-cut

enough figure and an obvious enough device, but so inseparable in Conrad (at his best, of course) is technique
from content that even the superficial consideration of
Marlow has led us into the inexpressible.

"Chance" is that rare thing, a work of fine spiritual
significance and a technical *tour de force*. It deserves for
itself the epithet "great" unqualified. The book itself is
a great book, not merely the product of a great writer.
The author has undertaken a spiritual revelation of extreme
subtlety. The book is pervaded by the air of fatality, and
the significance of the ramified conflict which is the "affair"
passes beyond the catastrophe of physical death to the
horror of spiritual annihilation. The subject, which may
be seen as the spiritual rescue of Flora de Barral from the
forces of darkness, from simple elimination by the evil in
the world (Conrad's sense of evil has never been more
intense than in this quiet, unmelodramatic story), which
all but suffocates and poisons her consciousness, sprawling
over her as a gigantic black slug might slime over a border
of flowers, is a solemn one. There can be nothing more
solemn in the world than the contemplation of a hair's-
breadth escape from spiritual obliteration. And yet the
book itself is not solemn. The book is not solemn in spite
of the fact that every ounce is got out of its extremely
solemn subject, *that* subject, which is so presented that all
its myriad overtones sound freely, unconstrained. And
this blessed lack of solemnity it owes to Conrad's exalted
sense of perspective which puts that solemn episode, that
little episode, which is nevertheless microcosmic in its meaning, exquisitely in its place in a world which it is fatal
to regard with solemnity. His great achievement in

132

" Chance " (and not in that book alone) is his just relating of a dreadful episode to the world as a whole without in the least robbing it of its own implicit horror.

But we were discussing Marlow in his elementary aspects, not Conrad's sensibility. And the immediate point was to show that Marlow was never the device of a novelist too lazy to work in another convention. In " Chance," if nowhere else, the difficulties of handling him are plain. They are magnificently vanquished, and the effect is, I believe, unique. To turn again to Henry James, who provides an extremely beautiful image of Marlow's part in the story, we have in him " a prolonged hovering flight of the subjective over the outstretched ground of the case exposed. We make out this ground but through the shadow cast by the flight, clarify it though the real author visibly reminds himself again and again that he must—all the more that, as if by some tremendous forecast of future applied science, the upper aeroplane causes another, as we have said, to depend from it and that one still another ; these dropping shadow after shadow, to the no small menace of intrinsic colour and form and whatever, upon the passive expanse."

Yet if Marlow is never elsewhere so hard to handle as he was in " Chance," in those other stories he is very necessary. From him in " Youth " springs that atmosphere of vital enthusiasm in reminiscence which is lacking in " The Shadow Line." In " Heart of Darkness " he is truly indispensable. For here, through his sensibility, we have the gradual revelation of a character whom we hardly meet

133

and whose death-bed taciturnity would have rendered the use of the third person impossible. The warped character of Kurtz, moreover, would, even had Conrad been able to manage it (which he would not have been), have turned a revelation of character by any interior method into grotesque fantasy ; for the whole world viewed through his eyes would have been a place of fantastic abomination, and also, written from his standpoint, there would be no contrast between actuality as perceived by normal eyes and the eyes of insanity. It would have been something like " The Cabinet of Dr. Caligari," only unbearably hideous and of a limited pathological interest. And, in any case, Conrad was not intent on describing Kurtz nor in revealing his precise mentality, but in rendering the sinister fatality of his environment ; and this is an aspect of life which interested him a great deal, which is never absent from his studies of Almayer, Willems, and other white men living in the East. The environment is made to work on Marlow himself until his flesh begins to creep. We remember his atavistic shudders at the sound of the reverberating drums, preparing us insidiously and with great subtlety for the dreadful revelation that is to come. In that way, and in that way only (remembering Conrad's limitations), can he give us the horror—the contrast between the man as he was and the man as he is—in a single sickening glimpse of truth. The method of interior revelation cannot give you the past and the present in a single phrase, for a man in his own consciousness is only what he is at the moment of being, at every moment of being ; and even the most poignant retrospective glance will be coloured by the subjective eye of his present state.

If " Chance " is a triumphant *tour de force,* " Under Western Eyes " is a flawed one. Here the narrator is not Marlow but his first cousin, a shore-going teacher of languages. And to me this book seems to fail because that schoolmaster is never made convincing as Marlow is always made convincing. He is too plainly, as Marlow never is, a device, and this in spite of Conrad's strenuous efforts at justification. Marlow is a plausible figure and his conversational powers are perfectly in character. He yarns on and on, and even when his yarning seems to get a little out of hand his actual speaking presence can be, and is, spot-lighted for a moment to banish the fleeting doubt of his existence. Marlow talks, and he is a good talker ; we understand that he has been a copious talker all his life, and there is no reason why he should not have been. You find talkers of genius in every profession ; but you do not find writers of genius like the teacher of languages who have waited until late middle-age before putting pen to paper and then do not realize the strength of their talents. You simply do not. And for me it is impossible to believe in that written account of the teacher of languages ; even without that inane prefatory remark : " To begin with I wish to disclaim the possession of those high gifts of imagination and expression which would have enabled my pen to create for the reader the personality of—— " etc. Somebody should have stopped Conrad from printing that sentence ; he was not after all alone. This little language teacher with all his shrewdness and insight into character does always remain a little pedagogue ; and from the beginning the reader has his potentialities summed up, potentialities which do not include the ability to write this kind of paragraph (opening the book almost at random) :

" The landing was prolonged into a bare corridor, right and left, desolate perspective of white and gold decoration without a strip of carpet. The very light, pouring through a large window at the end, seemed dusty ; and a solitary speck reposing on the balustrade of white marble—the silk top-hat of the great feminist—asserted itself extremely, black and glossy in all that crude whiteness."

That is not perfect, but it is genius. And it is plain that Marlow's cousin was not a genius, for all his excellent qualities.

The unpractised writer is always constrained. Conrad knew this, of course, and he is at pains to start his story with a most becoming stilted gravity. Our pedagogue might have begun the book, but he could never have finished it, for soon Conrad exalts him above himself and makes him write page on page of incandescent Conrad, plainly in the hope, on the assumption indeed, that, carried away by the unfolded tale, the reader will have no mind for the narrator's miraculous growth of wings. And if the pedagogue's part had consisted exclusively of straight-forward narration that would have been all right. He could have made his bow, set his ball rolling, and promptly sunk down into obscurity, the reader forgetting his exist-ence. But he does not sink down ; his narrative is only a part of his duty. As Conrad himself remarks of his genesis :

" In my desire to produce the effect of actuality it seemed to me indispensable to have an eye-witness of the trans-actions in Geneva. I needed a sympathetic friend for Miss

Haldin, who otherwise would have been too much alone and unsupported to be perfectly credible. She would have had no one to whom she could give a glimpse of her idealistic faith, of her great heart, and of her simple emotions."

And so the teacher of languages is not forgotten. In the first part of the book he pops up repeatedly, and later on he is seen to be an integral part of the story—Miss Haldin's moral support (for reasons of verisimilitude) and Miss Haldin's confidant (for verisimilitude and for technical reasons too, since by hook or by crook her secret thoughts must be conveyed to the reader). And each time he appears on the scene one remembers those splendid passages and mentally exclaims, " Oh no, not he ! " He is a character so perfectly realized, and that is nine-tenths of the trouble. Had Conrad left him nebulous and faceless it would have been impossible to feel strongly one way or the other about him ; but he is not vague ; on the contrary : he is drawn in the round ; he is beautifully definite in all his qualities and limitations. And because of this the splendour of his prose seems the more sharply out of character.

It is mainly that, as I see it, which makes " Under Western Eyes " inferior to " Chance " : in the one there is an excellent narrator and there is an excellent character, but the two are at odds ; in the other the narration springs naturally from the nature of the character. It is still magnificent, nevertheless. It is manifestly the work of a great writer and all that that implies. But the work of a great writer is not necessarily a great work, and in that distinction lies the difference between " Under Western Eyes " and " Chance," between " War and Peace " and

" Smoke." For a great novel, a great work of art, is the ultimate crystallization of the mind of a great artist, a consummation which it is given to few great artists to achieve.

Once this matter of the schoolmaster's rhetorical power is granted (and Conrad took it for granted) the handling of the narrative is masterly. It is like a brilliant argument founded on false premises. The treatment of the schoolmaster is not nearly so complex as the treatment of Marlow in " Chance," but it is almost as just and effective ; and the knitting together through him of the two main aspects of the story, the Razumov aspect (through Razumov's own narrative) and the Natalie Haldin aspect (through the friendship between the girl and the narrator) is contrived with a minimum of strain and with a fine effortlessness. The shape of the whole book, with the teacher of languages as the keystone, is considered and just—although, as we shall see later, far from perfect. The leading off with Razumov's narrative of a period of his life coming long before he met Miss Haldin, and the gradual working up to the point where that narrative merges into present reality, is a *tour de force* of the first order. If only Conrad could have killed off his characters as he so deftly killed off many others—Nostromo, Heyst, Captain Antony (poor Captain Antony, so ruthlessly sacrificed to an æsthetic pattern !), Peyroll (not quite so deftly)—we should indeed have a living image of the serpent with its tail in its mouth.

We find Conrad somewhat inanely protesting his lack of literary skill in another context, in " The Arrow of Gold " at that point where he introduces extracts from his

138

diary kept at the time of his first meeting with Dona Rita ;
it is a silly trick and quite unworthy of him. This particular instance also enables us to observe an excellent
example of Conrad's unsleeping vigilance over probabili-
ties, his endless preoccupation with verisimilitude which
keeps him as endlessly justifying every step he takes. To
quote Mr. Ford : " Before everything a story must convey
a sense of inevitability : that which happens in it must
seem to be the only thing that could have happened. Of
course a character may cry : ' If I had then acted differently
how different everything now would be.' The problem of
the author is to make his then action the only action that
character could have taken. It must be inevitable, because
of his character, because of his ancestry, because of past
illnesses or on account of the gradual coming together of
the thousand small circumstances by which Destiny, who
is inscrutable and august, will push us into one certain predicament." And this matter of justification, evident
enough in the rendering of the major actions of his characters, is pushed by Conrad with the scrupulousness of
genius into the smallest, most trivial points imaginable.

The ordinary novelist, if he wanted an excerpt from his
hero's diary, even if the hero were illiterate, would produce
it with little ado from some mysterious pocket and start
quoting. But Conrad knew perfectly well that M. George
(which is Conrad himself) would not in normal circumstances have kept a diary, being a young man of great
activity and little reflection ; and so we have to be shown
" the gradual coming together of the thousand small circumstances " which will push a man into a certain predicament
—the necessity of keeping a diary in this case. Here it is :

139

"Expression on paper has never been my forte. My life had been a thing of outward manifestations. I never had been secret or taciturn about my simple occupations which might have been foolish but had never required either caution or mystery. But in those four hours since midday a complete change had come over me. For good or evil I left that house committed to an enterprise that could not be talked about ; which would have appeared to many senseless and perhaps ridiculous, but was certainly full of risks, and, apart from that, commanded discretion on the ground of simple loyalty. It would not only close my lips, but it would to a certain extent cut me off from my usual haunts and from the society of my friends ; especially the light-hearted, young, harum-scarum kind. This was unavoidable. It was because I felt myself thrown back upon my own thoughts and forbidden to seek relief amongst other lives—it was perhaps only for that reason at first that I started an irregular fragmentary record of my days.

"I made these notes not so much to preserve the memory (one cared not for to-morrow then) but to help me to keep a better hold of the actuality."

There is our justification—all that for the sake of a few quoted pages ! But not for that alone, or the game would not have been worth the candle ; if that passage were justification for the diary-keeping episode and for nothing more it would be insupportable. But it is so worked into the texture of the main narrative that it not only justifies what is to follow, but also provides a further glimpse into M. George's mind—and, above all, provides us with the first, the very first intimation of what happened between

Mills, Blunt, Dona Rita, and himself in the interval between the close of chapter three and the opening of chapter four, between lunch and tea, that is—an important conference of the nature and upshot of which we know nothing until that hint of perils to come worked cunningly into the justification of the diary and connecting up with the highly allusive observations in the first of the two "notes" between which the story is suspended. The ordinary novelist would have taken to the diary without explanation. The more careful novelist would have paused to explain why his hero kept a diary at that time. The novelist of genius uses the explanation about the diary to provide the reader with some extremely important information—or vice versa. This is what is meant when we say that every word carries the story forward, which is more than rushing the narrative along at a spanking pace, which is in fact a continual contriving that every incidental phrase shall also have a *direct* bearing on the main business in hand.

That is Conrad in a nutshell, not the Conrad of the purple patches, but the supreme novelist, the teller of tales. Granted that one was familiar with the broad lines of " The Arrow of Gold " it should, I imagine, be possible to deduce from that passage the greater part of Conrad's technical greatness. It would be amusing to try.

As it is, however, this particular justification is to some extent spoilt. It is flawed by the phrase " expression on paper has never been my forte " which ruins the justification through excess of zeal. And there was no need for that phrase ; it is an entirely wanton trick. M. George is a young man of untried talents who might well have possessed the talent of expression ; and indeed, since he is none other than the youthful Conrad, he did, like a baton in his knapsack. The verisimilitude of the teacher of languages is spoilt in spite of his modest disclaimer. The verisimilitude of the diary is spoilt because of the disclaimer. It matters little in this case, however, since the diary is unimportant in itself and, by some curious trick of mind, one has no difficulty in dissociating the youthful writer of the diary from the mature writer of the whole story of which the diary is but a part.

At this time of life, it is of interest to note, Conrad seems to have amused himself extensively by turning up old diaries. One of them appears in " The Arrow of Gold " (1919), another in " The Shadow Line " (1917). Or he may have made them up, interesting himself simply in the diary as a technical device. In neither case is the device triumphant. Mr. Mégroz includes the one in " The Shadow Line " among Conrad's " few and unimportant lapses from credibility." His point is spoilt in the next breath, however, by the assertion that " There is no earthly reason for these notes. They are simply a continuation of the skipper's narrative." And so they are, so they are. . . . It is difficult to conceive what else they might have been. And they do flaw the story, too. But to say that there is " no earthly reason " for them is quite another matter.

In the first place to say of anything occurring in the work of an artist that " there is no earthly reason " for it is dangerous and almost certainly untrue. In the second place the reason for these notes in " The Shadow Line " is pretty obvious, and it is the same as the reason for the notes in " The Arrow of Gold." Both arise directly out of the problem of preserving the illusion round which we are circling in this chapter. There may not be sufficient reason, but " sufficient " is not a synonym for " earthly." For these notes are an attempt, an all too half-hearted attempt, it is true, to refresh the reader's faculty of credibility which Conrad evidently feared was suffering some strain. Not belief in the events themselves, oh no ; but belief in the narrator's memory.

M. George in " The Arrow of Gold " and the skipper in " The Shadow Line " have both of them been yarning on at some length, at great length, describing past events with their attendant atmosphere in detail of a most meticulous kind. And Conrad, with the problem of the maintenance of illusion ever alive to his mind, quite evidently asks himself whether the reader will not, at any moment now, be asking *him*self how on earth these two fellows, M. George and the skipper of the *Otago*, expect anyone to believe that they could remember all that detail after so many years. This was for Conrad the cause of perfectly legitimate concern. Mr. Ford, as usual, has a relevant paragraph, with particular reference to the reporting of a character's speech verbatim : " To pretend that any character or any author writing directly can remember whole speeches with all their words for a matter of twenty-four hours, let alone twenty-four years, is absurd." He adds a little later that " This was one of the matters as to which the writer was more uncompromising that Conrad . . . Conrad indeed later arrived at the conclusion that, a novel being in the end a matter of convention . . . you might as well stretch convention a little farther, and postulate that your author or your narrator is a person of prodigious memory for the spoken." That is evident enough throughout the greater part of Conrad's output, notably in the Marlow appearances. But in these two books, " The Arrow of Gold " and " The Shadow Line," he seems to have taken panic, to have feared for the integrity of his illusion, and to have searched wildly round for something to bolster it up. And the device of the diary is hit upon. For even though only a few pages are quoted from it directly, the reader may, if he at all troubles his head about such matters, feel throughout the remainder of the narrative that the diary is always *there* even when it is not directly quoted from, and the plethora of reminiscent detail may be conveniently accounted for by the fact that the narrator can always dip into the diary to refresh his memory.

And that is excellent. As a reason it is unassailable. The trouble is not that " there is no earthly reason for it " but that the device is radically unsatisfactory.

It is unsatisfactory because if that diary is to have an air of verisimilitude it must be a pretty dud affair from the evocative point of view ; the events recorded in it will be events sketchily, even if brilliantly, rendered, which is a waste of good material. If, on the other hand, you are determined, as Conrad was determined, never to waste good material and to make the most of everything the alleged diary will read like a book and not like a diary at all. This dilemma Conrad ignored. He was evidently conscious of it, for his diaries both start off in a sober and matter of fact manner ; but he turns his back on it almost at once and the diaries, like the teacher of languages, grow wings. In both these instances he would indeed have done better to have suppressed his youthful notes and, taking the novel as a convention, postulated his narrators as persons " of prodigious memory." Only a very few readers would have noticed anything at all fishy, and a reader who thinks enough about the novel as a technical problem to notice such a thing will be sympathetically disposed and understanding in face of a novelist as scrupulous as Conrad. As things are, the diary sticks out, as they say, a mile. It causes people who never give a thought to technique to trip up and regard it as so much wanton idiocy, and in the breasts of those who take an interest in the problems of the novelist it arouses pity, which is the last thing Conrad wanted.

All these lapses were due to excess of zeal, and we have considered them not for the sake of noting lapses but for the sake of the light they shed on the problems which Conrad had to face, only the most elementary problems hitherto, and of the scrupulousness with which he faced them. But there are also times when this scrupulousness failed, and the consequent falls from grace are the more disconcerting for their rarity. In the two diary episodes he seems to have panicked, for a moment losing faith in his convention and hesitating fatally. But there are also occasions when an access of panic would have improved matters considerably. In the unfinished novel, " Suspense," in which Conrad achieves a limpidity and an ease of manner which verges on the sheer loveliness of a Mozart *Serenade*, one comes with a sense of shock (shock is not the word, for the discovery is gradual ; with rapidly growing uneasiness, then) on the development of Adèle's long narration to Cosmo, a monologue of Marlowesque proportions, quite unsuited in length, detail, consistency, and uninterrupted flow, with time, place, and particularly character. We do not mind Marlow holding forth for hours together ; he has the air of a born narrator, and his friends assemble for the sake of his yarns. But the heroine of " Suspense " is not at home in the sustained, consecutive monologue ; it is doubtful if any woman is. In the most propitious circumstances she could never have given that performance ; and the circumstances were indeed far from that. She would have wanted to hear more from Cosmo ; she would have interrupted herself a thousand times ; and, in any case, with the spectre of that husband lurking behind the doors and at any moment liable to interrupt her narrative, her tongue would have been paralysed. I go into detail for the look of the thing, but the chief fact, and the only one that really matters, is that an oration of this kind is hopelessly out of character. The " Suspense " narrative is very bad indeed. It is impossible to criticize it whole-heartedly, since the novel is unfinished and one has no means of knowing whether Conrad would have worked over that scene again. One imagines not, since the fragment that we have is highly polished ; and also Conrad has quite evidently got the bit between his teeth, and on the rare occasions on which this happens there is no holding him, neither by sense nor by reason. He desired to give the reader some information essential to the understanding of the story and the characters ; he wanted to get it over quickly, and get it over quickly he did without reference to any elements but time and space. He had a tendency to forget himself in this

was the outcome of Conrad's temperament and make-up, but it is also interesting to note that despite his avoidance of any form of the interior monologue as a rule there were moments which for purposes of dramatic effect cried out for such treatment, moments when, for some reason or another, Conrad did feel intimately in touch with the train of thought passing through a given character's mind, and could image it to himself. In certain works, in " Nostromo," for instance, his method—in that case the direct exterior method—enables him, with careful manipulation, to change his standpoint for a moment and dip into a character's consciousness when he felt it could be done with effect. But there is one very curious lapse in a book written in the first person, in " The Nigger of the Narcissus," which is worth quoting as an indication of a temptation to which Conrad must frequently have found himself exposed, in spite of his subjective outlook. It suggests, indeed, that in the actual glow of composition his mind was raised out of itself and that he did have a fleeting objective vision of the unseen and unseeable which in sober moments was denied him. This particular moment in " The Nigger of the Narcissus " seems to me really very extraordinary, both for the light it throws on Conrad's mind and as an example of a really atrocious and unpardonable lapse. The story is told in the first person throughout by one of the sailors concerned, and because of this Conrad is free to speculate and comment to his heart's desire, his imperative privilege, of which here as everywhere he makes full use ; but if he is free to speculate, all objective description must plainly be done from the outside only. The narrator, one of the sailors concerned, can have no *knowledge* of what is going on in the minds of the rest of the crew ; he can only guess, just as Marlow can only guess. And yet in this book, which Conrad thought so highly of, which was not written until he had a firm notion of the various principles of his art, one finds this :

(The scene is the negro's cabin, and the cook is alone with Jimmy. The narrator of the story is not even an eye-witness of the scene ; and the cook, into whose mind he projects himself so whole-heartedly, deserves no more special attention than any other of the characters.)

"Jimmy drank a gulp of tea, hurriedly, as though he had stolen it and shrank under the blanket, edging away towards the bulkhead. The cook got up, closed the door, then sat down again and said distinctly :

" ' Whenever I poke my galley fire I think of you chaps —swearing, stealing, lying, and worse—as if there were no such thing as another world. . . . Not bad fellows either, in a way,' he conceded slowly ; then, after a pause of regretful musing, he went on in a resigned tone : ' Well, well. They will have a hot time of it. Hot ! Did I say ? The furnaces of one of them White Star boats ain't nothing to it.'

"He kept very quiet for a while. There was a great stir in his brain ; an addled vision of bright outlines ; an exciting row of rousing songs and groans of pain. He suffered, enjoyed, admired, approved. He was delighted, frightened, exalted—as on that evening (the only time in his life—twenty-seven years ago ; he loved to recall the number of years) when as a young man he had—through keeping bad company—become intoxicated in an East-end music-hall. A tide of sudden feeling swept him clean out

149

of his body. He soared. He contemplated the secret of the hereafter. It commended itself to him. It was excellent ; he loved it, himself, all hands, and Jimmy. His heart overflowed with tenderness, with comprehension, with the desire to meddle, with anxiety for the soul of that black man, with the pride of possessed eternity, with the feeling of might. . . ."

And so it goes on, becoming ever more particular, and all of it indefensible. No postulating of conventions can excuse that sin, which is itself a sin against convention. It is as bad an example of a novelist cheating and at the same time cutting his own throat as will ever be found within the covers of a book. " Where on earth have you got all that from ? " we cry with increasing irritation. And for once there is no answer. Even the man who never appeared in slippers, who, figuratively speaking, always had his boots on, is caught nodding at times. It did not happen often outside the earliest books of all, and it seems to me probable that this lapse and others in " The Nigger of the Narcissus " are due to the fact that at the time of writing Conrad, although his instincts were strong, had not got them clearly before his eyes as principles. This kind of lapse is hinted at again in " Nostromo " very slightly once or twice, but never after that ; and it seems to me by no means without significance that the friendship and collaboration with Ford Madox Ford began soon after the completion of the " Nigger." This, I may be forgiven for emphasizing, is not to suggest that Conrad's technical dexterity is due bodily to Ford. On the contrary ; there are signs even in " Almayer's Folly " that Conrad has thought a great deal about the craft of fiction. But he is in the earlier books still muddled in the application of his ideas ; the whole first person convention in " The Nigger of the Narcissus " is several times misused. Scenes are described at which the narrator was not present—that little scene between Jimmy and the cook, part of which we have just witnessed, is an instance. But after that book there is no large-scale clumsiness. It is plain that Conrad has more completely ordered his ideas, and the signs point to the collaboration as the turning point, and to all the talk it must have involved, talk which sharpens nebulous ideas as nothing else can.

" Nostromo," which is perhaps the richest novel Conrad ever wrote, is done in the third person, and for nine-tenths of it in the direct method. In view of Conrad's particular limitations its technique is of extreme interest. Throughout, the characters are described from the standpoint of an outside observer, the author himself, who does not take omniscience upon himself, but who undertakes to reveal all he has to reveal by a delicate and just rendering of what is visible to the eye. For most of these characters this treatment is adequate, and the book has that fine, clear-cut surface which is inseparably associated with this method when beautifully exploited—as, for instance, Maupassant exploited it. The necessity to reveal the secrets of the heart by the rendering of conduct, gesture, appearance, and speech results when it is well done in the finest of fine edges. Above all it makes for brevity, for the swift, incisive glance. It fails only when the shades of feeling and sensibility are so fine and crowding that no human

body or behaviour is capable of expressing them, as in
" Chance."   But in " Nostromo," apart from the Capataz
de Cargadores himself, there is no call for such subtlety ;
and the cool, unclouded, one might say rarified, exterior
treatment serves.   Mrs. Gould, Charles Gould, Antonia,
Don José de Avellanos, and all the rest save Nostromo and
Martin Decoud are all unambiguous creatures who can be
made to reveal themselves with the help of genius in the
onlooker.   And one of the joys of this treatment may be
found at the very end of the book when, in two words, in
a flash, all one's knowledge and understanding of Mrs.
Gould is crystallized.   Conrad was forbidden by his convention to unveil her soul directly.   She must speak.   And
a certain phrase of hers coming after a thousand small
speeches and silent agonies is decisive, clinching, all-illuminating.   Mrs. Gould, in almost the last words she utters in
that story, is finally " got in."   Nostromo is dying ; the
magnificent Capataz de Cargadores is gone, leaving his
trail of destruction behind him.   " Material Interests "
have claimed their victims, old Viola dead over his bible
in the lighthouse, Linda, racked and wild-eyed, tending the
light, and Giselle, fled from her fear and that dreadful rock
of passions :

" ' Pray send at once somebody for my carriage,' spoke
Mrs. Gould from within her hood.   Then turning to
Giselle Viola, ' Come nearer me, child , come closer.   We
will wait here.'

" Giselle Viola, heartbroken and childlike, her face
veiled in her falling hair, crept up to her side.   Mrs. Gould
slipped her hand through the arm of the unworthy daughter
of old Viola, the immaculate republican, the hero without

a stain. Slowly, gradually, as a withered flower droops, the head of the girl, who would have followed a thief to the end of the world, rested on the shoulder of Dona Emilia, the first lady of Sulaco, the wife of the Senor Administrador of the San Tomé mine. And Mrs. Gould, feeling her suppressed sobbing, nervous and excited, had the first and only moment of bitterness in her life. It was worthy of Dr. Monygham himself:

" ' Console yourself, child. Very soon he would have forgotten you for his treasure.'

" ' Senora, he loved me. He loved me,' Giselle whispered, despairingly. ' He loved me as no one has ever been loved before.'

" ' I have been loved too,' Mrs. Gould said in a severe tone."

. . . "I have been loved too"—in that single phrase coming at the most poignant spot in time of the whole novel, coming in the silence of desolation on the heels of catastrophe with the dust still hanging over the ruins—in that phrase we have the final, definite, unambiguous revelation of Mrs. Gould's own tragedy, already suggested. The sentence itself is sufficient ; but occurring where it does occur it conjures up suddenly a panoramic vision of the past, of the freshness of youth and lightness, into a scene from which youth and lightness have been absent for so long that they have been forgotten, that they might never have existed. This ultimate crystallization of a complex mood could have been approached in other ways, but by no other method than the method employed in " Nostromo " could it have been reached exactly.

I spoke of the method of " Nostromo," and wrote, away from the book, to the best of my memory ; but so vivid was the memory of certain scenes, so intimate the acquaintance with the states of mind of certain of the characters, that I was forced to take up the book to make sure that Conrad does, as I have said, write always from the standpoint of the outside but not omniscient observer. The scenes between Charles and Emilia Gould in Italy before their marriage were exceptionally vivid in the mind, so vivid that it seemed impossible for any man to impress such shades of feeling and apprehension on the reader's mind without going behind one or other of his characters. But on opening the book the scene was there, and Conrad does not go behind ; and so perfectly do these pages illustrate the power of a novelist to reveal the depths and subtleties of a character's mind purely by rendering their external aspects that a page or so cries out for quotation. Perhaps more than anything else this kind of thing gives the measure of Conrad's sensuous approach and the extraordinary fineness of his senses :

" The two young people had met in Lucca. After that meeting Charles Gould visited no mines, though they went together in a carriage, once, to see some marble quarries, where the work resembled mining in so far that it also was the tearing of the raw material of treasure from the earth. Charles Gould did not open his heart to her in any set speeches. He simply went on acting and thinking in her sight. This is the true method of sincerity. One of his frequent remarks was, ' I think sometimes that poor father takes a wrong view of that San Tomé business.' And they discussed that opinion long and earnestly, as if they could influence a mind across half the globe ; but in reality they discussed it because the sentiment of love can enter into any subject and live ardently in remote phrases. For this natural reason these discussions were precious to Mrs. Gould in her engaged state. Charles feared that Mr. Gould, senior, was wasting his strength and making himself ill by his efforts to get rid of the Concession. ' I fancy that this is not the kind of handling it requires,' he mused aloud, as if to himself. And when she wondered frankly that a man of character should devote his energies to plotting and intrigues, Charles would remark, with a gentle concern that understood her wonder, ' You must not forget that he was born there.'

" She would set her quick mind to work on that, and then make the inconsequent retort, which he accepted as perfectly sagacious, because, in fact, it was so—

" ' Well, and you ? You were born there too.'

" He knew his answer.

" ' That's different. I've been away ten years. Dad never had such a long spell ; and it was more than thirty years ago.'

" She was the first person to whom he opened his lips after receiving the news of his father's death.

" ' It has killed him ! ' he said.

" He had walked straight out of town with the news, straight out before him in the noonday sun on the white road, and his feet had brought him face to face with her in the hall of the ruined palazzo, a room magnificent and naked, with here and there a long strip of damask, black with damp and age, drooping straight down on a bare panel of the wall. It was furnished with exactly one gilt armchair, with a broken back, and an octagon columnar stand bearing a heavy marble vase ornamented with sculptured masks and garlands of flowers, and cracked from top to bottom. Charles Gould was dusty with the white dust of the road lying on his boots, on his shoulders, on his cap with two peaks. Water dripped from under it all over his face, and he grasped a thick oaken cudgel in his bare right hand.

" She went very pale under the roses of her big straw hat, gloved, swinging a clear sunshade, caught just as she was going out to meet him at the bottom of the hill, where three poplars stand near the wall of a vineyard.

" ' It has killed him ! ' he repeated. ' He ought to have had many years yet. We are a long-lived family.'

" She was too startled to say anything ; he was contemplating with a penetrating and motionless stare the cracked marble urn as though he had resolved to fix its shape for ever in his memory. It was only when, turning suddenly to her, he blurted out twice, ' I've come to you— I've come straight to you——,' without being able to finish his phrase, that the great pitifulness of that lonely and tormented death in Costaguana came to her with the full force of its misery. He caught hold of her hand, raised it to his lips, and at that she dropped her parasol to pat him on the cheek, murmured ' Poor boy,' and began to dry her eyes under the downward curve of her hat-brim, very small in her simple, white frock, almost like a lost child crying in the degraded grandeur of the noble hall, while he stood by her, again perfectly motionless in the contemplation of the marble urn.

" Afterwards they went out for a long walk, which was silent till he exclaimed suddenly—

" ' Yes. But if he had only grappled with it in a proper way ! ' "

It continues thus. It speaks for itself. It is impossible to conceive of a more exacting way of doing that kind of scene than the way Conrad has chosen, the way forced on him by the need for consistency within the covers of a book. It is impossible to imagine a way as effective when it is followed as Conrad follows it here. It makes one a little tired of the deep, stertorous delving of other novelists into consciousnesses which they do not reveal a tenth as fully as Conrad does here, standing outside. It vividly recalls Conrad's own phrase about " The Return " : " I should like to confess my surprise on finding that notwithstanding all its apparatus of analysis the story consists for the most part of physical impressions : impressions of sound and sight. . . ."

But if this kind of treatment is enough for the Goulds, the Violas, and the Spaniards, Conrad found it inadequate for a proper presentation of Nostromo. He finds it necessary to comment on Nostromo, to suggest. And this he achieves with no flaw in his consistency by making Martin Decoud write a long letter home to his sister in Paris in the course of which the character of Nostromo is speculatively explored. And in the true Conrad manner this letter is made to serve more than one purpose. It is written in a pocket-book in the heat of the street fighting, and it becomes in a way symbolic.

Conrad, nevertheless, is not satisfied with this, and at one point of the story he gets behind Nostromo in a way which

157

strikes me as neither effective nor justifiable. Nostromo is alone in the darkness of the bay, with no one to whom he may reveal himself in conversation ; but it seems to me that it would have been a great deal better had Conrad cut straight from his departure from the Isabels to his re-appearance in the town, and later, in his own words, in his confession to Gisella perhaps, have recalled the substance of his meditations hanging between life and death. This would have avoided the direct revelation of Nostromo's mind, which is out of place in that story, which Conrad handles very badly in any case, and at the same time have brought the forgotten atmosphere of those breathless nights of romantic adventure down into the humdrum, furtive present. As for Decoud's interior monologue preparatory to his suicide—it seems to me that Conrad made a mistake here too. We know enough of Decoud already to guess at the motives which drove him to the fatal act without this somewhat lurid picture of his state of mind, and the image of the deserted island, the empty boat, the missing pieces of silver taken to weight his body down, would have brought the horror of the situation memorably home.

By now we should have a fair idea of the usual methods by which Conrad revealed the minds of his characters or retained his freedom of comment on them. They are methods born of his own temperamental qualities and limitations ; for although we have stressed up to now his particular lack, the quality of invention, of psychological synthesis, these methods, and perhaps the method of " Nostromo " above all, depend equally on the presence of

rare qualities of vision and apprehension. They saved him
trouble in that they enabled him to do what would otherwise have been impossible, or all but ; and yet the few
examples we have taken should indicate to some extent the
obstacles which they raised in his path and the exalted state
of mental alertness which, in a novelist of conscience, must
ceaselessly be imposed like an iron frame on the impulsive
spirit. The conflict is so fierce that in perfection the frame
and the spirit glow white and are fused. And that, after
all, is the main justification for rules of any kind in art, the
empirical justification. A flame untrammelled is large,
wavering, and yellow ; a flame confined is steady and
white. Sometimes the flame escapes through a flaw in the
confining mantle with a corresponding loss of incan-
descence.

There remains an approach on which so far we have not
touched. It is suggested as early as " Almayer's Folly "
in the treatment of Babalatchi and Lakamba, who are the
two living creatures in that book (it is interesting to note
that Mr. Garnett, to whom Conrad's readers owe so much,
was above all struck by Babalatchi in that book ; and one
may wonder, indeed, whether he would have passed the
thing for publication had it lacked Babalatchi, Lakamba,
and their vitalizing influence on the story) ; we find hints
of it in " An Outpost of Progress " ; and certain of the
minor characters in " Nostromo "—Montero and Hirsch,
for instance—carry the suggestion too. But in these early
books the approach, the ironic approach, to which I refer,
is used less consciously as a technical device than as a spon-

taneous method of illumination. There are passages in
" Almayer's Folly " which hold more promise than the
whole of the rest of the book. A man who in his first book
can write this sort of thing is a marked man :

" Lakamba roused himself from his apathy with an
appearance of having grasped the situation at last.

" ' Babalatchi,' he called briskly, giving him a slight
kick.

" ' Ada Tuan ! I am listening.'

" ' If the Orang Blanda come here, Babalatchi, and take
Almayer to Batavia to punish him for smuggling gun-
powder, what will he do, do you think ? '

" ' I do not know, Tuan.'

" ' You are a fool,' commented Lakamba exultingly.
' He will tell them where the treasure is, so as to find mercy.
He will.'

" Babalatchi looked up at his master and nodded his
head with by no means a joyful surprise. He had not
thought of this ; there was a new complication.

" ' Almayer must die,' said Lakamba decisively, ' to
make our secret safe. He must die quietly, Babalatchi.
You must do it.'

" Babalatchi assented and rose wearily to his feet. ' To-
morrow ? ' he asked.

" ' Yes ; before the Dutch come. He drinks much
coffee,' answered Lakamba, with seeming irrelevancy.

" Babalatchi stretched himself yawning, but Lakamba,
in the flattering consciousness of a knotty problem solved
by his own unaided intellectual efforts, grew suddenly very
wakeful.

" ' Babalatchi,' he said to the exhausted statesman,

'fetch the box of music the white captain gave me. I cannot sleep.'

" At this order a deep shade of melancholy settled upon Babalatchi's features. He went reluctantly behind the curtain and soon reappeared carrying in his arms a small hand-organ, which he put down on the table with an air of deep dejection. Lakamba settled himself comfortably in his armchair.

" ' Turn, Babalatchi, turn,' he murmured, with closed eyes.

" Babalatchi's hand grasped the handle with the energy of despair, and as he turned, the deep gloom on his countenance changed into an expression of hopeless resignation. Through the open shutter the notes of Verdi's music floated out on the great silence over the river and forest. Lakamba listened with closed eyes and a delighted smile ; Babalatchi turned, at times dozing off and swaying over, then catching himself up in a great fright with a few quick turns of the handle. Nature slept in an exhausted repose after the fierce turmoil, while under the unsteady hand of the statesman of Sambir the Trovatore fitfully wept, and bade good-bye to his Leonore again and again in a mournful round of tearful and endless iteration."

Although that passage verges on the knockabout and is not perfectly in place in the story, it indicates a power of a valuable kind, a power which enters into a great deal of Conrad's writing, but which in " The Secret Agent " is made to serve as the basis of a consistent method of presentation. It is a method which, granted the necessary ironic flair in the author, for long passages runs of itself, but which, at times, raises difficulties of an exceptional order. In overcoming these difficulties and thereby retaining his consistency Conrad achieved what may have been the greatest of all his purely technical feats, although certain weaknesses in construction, various loose ends left lying about (the Assistant Commissioner, for instance, is left unceremoniously hanging in the air), rob the book of perfection. It is a method dictated by the necessity we have already examined, and it allows the author a freedom of action unusually extensive. He is free to comment, free to dip into the minds of all or any of his characters, free to be as subjective as he likes and as objective as he likes. That is a tall order indeed, but it has been done, and by what I should like to call, taking a hint from Mr. Curle, the method of ironic perspective.

To appreciate this feat at all adequately it is necessary to visualize the task with which Conrad found himself faced. The story to be told is a reconstruction of the Greenwich Park explosion, the story, suggested by Ford Madox Ford, of the attempted outrage by a semi-idiot urged on by his *agent provocateur* of a brother-in-law who was afterwards murdered by his wife—Stevie, Mr. Verloc, and Winnie Verloc. In the end, for æsthetic purposes, Winnie Verloc is made to commit suicide, when actually, according to Mr. Ford, she was " allowed to escape by the police."

That is the germ of the book. The characters to be illuminated are, most of them, drab—Stevie, the Verlocs, Winnie Verloc's mother, a foreign diplomat, an assortment of anarchists, a police inspector. Apart from the Assistant Commissioner of Police there is not a single character in the book with whom Conrad could feel in intellectual sympathy or into the everyday workings of whose mind Conrad, with his particular limitations, could be expected to enter. But Conrad desired not only to illuminate these people ; he proposed to show the whole affair from a particular standpoint, which at once rules out the " Nostromo " method. In other books a Marlow served this purpose, but to introduce Marlow into this story evidently seemed to him out of the question, and not among all these characters and their likely associates could there be found a mind sufficiently detached, sufficiently perceptive, sufficiently literate, even, to play Marlow to the Verlocs— unless, of course, from the Assistant Commissioner's angle, which would demand machinery far too cumbersome for its work. Plainly, then, the narrative must be offered by the author himself, that is impersonally. Yet how, in this convention, will Conrad be able to strike an attitude, to have his say about the characters and their affairs ? How, moreover, if he does strike an attitude, the attitude of an outside observer, will he be able to combine with this indulgence frequent raids into the enemy country, into the mind now of this character, now of that ? This, broadly speaking, is the problem which confronted Conrad as he contemplated the broken story of that abortive outrage. The triumphant solution is the book itself.

It is here that Conrad turns his ironic cast of mind to good account. Although in his book Mr. Curle is interested in Conrad's irony chiefly from the human point of view, he realizes the distinctiveness of the ironic treatment of " The Secret Agent " clearly enough to say that it is " more an artistic than a philosophic attitude," and here he gets very warm. But since he has not perceived the *necessity* which drove Conrad to use that particular method for that particular book he sheers off on to another trail, getting, as they say, colder and colder. The necessity we have already considered ; and it is the necessity which in other books drove Conrad to Marlow, in others to the exploitation of the first person singular—*that* necessity, together with the fact that both these methods seemed to him out of the question in this context. It is the necessity which made Conrad himself confess that " Even the purely artistic purpose, that of applying an ironic method to a subject of this kind, was formulated with deliberation and in the earnest belief that ironic treatment alone would enable me to say all I felt I would have to say in scorn as well as in pity."

" . . . all I felt I would have to say. . . ." That, by the way, is the only admission in the whole of Conrad of his need for freedom of comment on the supposition of which we have based so much.

Mr. Curle also speaks of a certain unity, a certain perspective, to be gained from viewing men and affairs from an ironical standpoint, and that, of course, is true. It accounts for Conrad's use of irony in other contexts (not always legitimate, I think), and it partly explains his use of it in " The Secret Agent "—but only partly. For Mr. Curle by " perspective " quite plainly means a human perspective, a universal perspective, the perspective of a man contemplating his fellow creatures ; Marlow's perspective. And although this Marlow's perspective is a dominant feature of all Conrad's writing, including " The Secret Agent," what is more to the point in that book is another kind of perspective altogether which itself contains the Marlow's perspective (also achieved by that same irony, which thus in this book serves a double purpose) to help in the illumination of the characters once they are, by the æsthetic perspective, put into a position for illumination. It is a matter of Chinese boxes.

The freedom and flexibility granted Conrad by the deliberate formulation of this method fully equals and possibly surpasses that granted him by Marlow. In effect the two methods are similar. In " Chance," with his series of reporters, Conrad puts the story at various removes from himself, never at less than one remove, through Marlow ; with the ironic treatment he puts it at one remove from reality. The whole affair is isolated, as it were, cut off from the run of normal existence and placed under a glass bell which, according to the angle of the incident light, has a more or less distorting effect on the objects it covers. That is the ironic haze. And this interposition of a barrier between the affair under consideration and the surrounding actuality does away with the necessity for adherence to any realistic convention, provided, always provided, that the whole affair in all its multitudinous aspects is viewed through the glass, is, in short, subjected to the ironic treatment. That is the convention, and so long as that convention is stuck to, the narrator has, in every other direction, untrammelled freedom of action.

The snag in the method is that although for a greater part of the time the characters on view are unsympathetic and easy game for irony, there are occasions when it is desirable to show a slice of life in its nakedness in order to arouse a straightforward emotion of simple humanity in the breast of the reader. And then, of course, there is the great peril of the distorting glass obtruding itself unduly between the reader and reality, robbing the passage of its sought effect . . . or, what would be more likely to happen, the novelist, yielding to the impulse of a moment, might risk lifting the glass to take a surreptitious glance underneath. He would thereby ruin his illusion. And the brilliance of Conrad's achievement in this book is the way in which by the most felicitous manipulation of light he renders his glass now more distorting, now less, so that on certain occasions (notably when the most sympathetic character in the book, Winnie Verloc, is required to move the reader to a straightforward emotion of pity for her desolation) the light is so contrived that there seems to be no glass : the effect is similar to that of those peculiar shop windows which at first sight invite the passer-by to casual larceny, but which, to a closer look, yield the secret of their cunning dispositions. And so it is with " The Secret Agent," a book which contains some of the most actual description and rendering in the whole of Conrad, yet all conditioned by the ironic convention. The fact of this convention enables Conrad to change his position as often as he likes and to comment at will, provided always that he remains on the outside of the glass bell. The flawless consistency with which it is upheld makes a reality which seems to be the only reality (since in the whole book there is no glimpse of undoctored reality to render possible a fatal comparison), but which is only the artificial reality of that book.

VII

A FREQUENT objection to preoccupation with that aspect of the novel which formed the matter of our last chapter is that it is a mechanical aspect, one which in no way depends upon the divine spark of genius, and one which may be studied to as much advantage in the works of a competent hack novelist as in the works of an artist. About that objection there is something insidiously plausible, yet it seems to me false. It is a matter of degree ; the calls which the artist makes upon himself are so much more exacting than anything expected from his inferiors, the ceaseless struggle to get the last ounce out of his subject and at the same time to keep the structure firm, lend to his most elementary technical devices a certain grandeur and significance over and above their mere face value. And the by no means infrequent failures of an artist in these elementary matters, failures of the kind which we have already noticed as occurring in Conrad's work, plainly suggest that such things may be less mechanical than they seem.

It is possible that the aspects touched on in the last chapter are all of a kind that can, by taking pains, be mastered by anybody at all capable of telling a story. They are certainly aspects which could be taught, as the groundwork of painting and composition can be taught ; which would be taught if people, including writers, cared enough about literature to demand of its practitioners a certain training. But there are also things which cannot be taught, subtler matters altogether, and coming under the vague head of inspiration. And even in our consideration of the ground-work we were pushed once or twice over the poorly-defined boundary between craft and art. In discussing Marlow, for instance, we found that at some point or other he ceased to be plain scaffolding and became an integral factor in what I called Conrad's contrapuntal treatment of his subjects, the super-augmented effect.

An important part of this contrapuntal treatment has been christened by Ford Madox Ford, by far its ablest exponent, the device of the time-shift ; and in his own study of Conrad the employment of this device as an aid to fidelity in rendering is so sufficiently indicated that there is little point in going into it here at any length. But Mr. Ford only touches on the time-shift as a device to break down the forced unnaturalness of the strictly chronological narrative. Speaking of that very book (" Joseph Conrad : A Personal Remembrance ") he explains that it is composed " exactly on the lines of the formula that Conrad and the writer evolved. For it became very early evident to us that what was the matter with the Novel, and the British novel in particular, was that it went straight forward, whereas in your gradual making acquaintanceship with your fellows you never do go straight forward. You meet an English gentleman at your golf club. He is beefy, full of health, the moral of a boy from an English Public School of the finest type. You discover, gradually, that he is hopelessly neurasthenic, dishonest in matters of small change, but unexpectedly self-sacrificing, a dreadful liar but a most painfully careful student of lepidoptera and, finally, from the public prints, a bigamist who was once, under another name, hammered on the Stock Exchange. . . . Still, there he is, a beefy, full-fed fellow, moral of an English Public School product.   To get such a man in fiction you could not begin at the beginning and work his life chronologically to the end.   You must first get him in with a strong impression, and then work backwards and forwards over his past. . . . That theory at least we gradually evolved."

And that will do for that.   The matter is gone into so justly in that book that any elaboration of the theory here, of that particular aspect of it, could be no more than a clumsy paraphrase.   It is not an all-embracing theory. There are times when the novelist must begin at the beginning ; but then he will be ruled by a particular purpose which was never Conrad's purpose.

The ability to work in that way was, although he may not consciously have realized it, part of Conrad's own original equipment, and with " Almayer's Folly " itself the method may be seen already in action.   The spirit there is willing, the flesh weak, and the result in consequence clumsy.   But it is only the execution which is poor ; the principle is excellent, and it allows us to see Conrad in his first novel of all boldly striking out to get Almayer in with a strong first impression as he stands on his verandah by the river at Sambir, then working back over his disreputable past until we are brought right up to the present with the arrival of Dain.

There are, however, other even more important aspects of this discursive treatment which Mr. Ford does not touch upon, although from his own novels it is plain that he is perfectly well aware of them and relies on them very considerably for his own effects. It is an aid not only to the presentation of the novelist's subject in its proper light and so to getting the last ounce out of the subject, but also to getting the last ounce out of every word and sentence, every paragraph and episode, by multiplying their duties. It is in this matter that Conrad's highest genius lies, in the significant arrangement of facts. He lacked what I have called the power of psychological synthesis ; but in the power of formal synthesis he is, at his best, unsurpassable.

With straightforward chronological narration each paragraph, save by accident or luck, is doing one thing and one thing only ; each paragraph, each sentence, each incident recorded. There are no overtones ; there is no diffused radiance. In the normal chronological narrative, beginning at the beginning and ending at the end, the beginning and the end in time, the contribution of each sentence to the total effect is no more than its own face value. Each sentence is no more than a statement of the fact expressed by it. This is a waste of space and it makes for thinness of texture, no matter how complex and decorated the individual sentences may be.

The trouble is that at any given moment in the story the reader is aware only of what he *knows*, of what has already been told him in a series of direct statements. At a given point of the story, in other words, all that the reader's mind has to work upon is what he knows of the characters and their histories up to a corresponding point in their lives. The rest is a blank ; and he can only speculate as to how the affair will develop judging from the natures and behaviour of the protagonists as so far exposed. Of all that comes after that given moment he is oblivious ; of all the contributory factors the author may yet have hidden up his sleeve, factors which may radically develop, inhibit, or otherwise condition the behaviour of the characters and influence their fates, he knows nothing at all. He is, in a word, completely in the dark. And it is the business of the author to illuminate, not to shadow.

The only excuse for leaving the reader in the dark about any part of the story is the need for the element of suspense. And the more the novelist can base his suspense not on curiosity as to what will physically happen next, but on curiosity as to his characters' reactions to any events that may occur, the less need is there for him to keep his readers in the dark as to the main lines of his affair. In the hands of Conrad, indeed, where the chief interest lies in the minds of the characters, some preliminary knowledge of their ultimate fates may and should act as the necessary spur ; for if these characters are well done, and if the reader's interest is adequately aroused, it is plain that the spectacle of the characters engaged in a struggle the rough outline of which he already knows will prove as powerful a stimulant to his curiosity as the most ominous ending to an instalment of a boy's serial story where curiosity is fed on adventure in the abstract, not on what adventure does to people's minds.

Conrad never took this theory to its perfectly logical

conclusion, by presenting the reader with the catastrophe on page one or thereabouts. Nor is it to be understood that the broken method of narration, save in certain circumstances, is primarily conditioned by the problem of holding the reader's interest ; that aspect of it is incidental. What it does do, much more importantly, is to bring about an extreme closeness of texture very satisfying to the adult mind and also to pervade the parts of the story with the atmosphere, the flavour, of the whole. The result is that at any given moment in the narrative the reader is aware of more than he actually knows.

In addition to this the broken method, which, employed in a simple romance of adventure would certainly be putting the cart before the horse, but which in any kind of psychological study has many advantages (since here the cart has been transmogrified into the horse), has the great merit of eliminating irrelevant distractions. For in a novel of the kind which Conrad wrote the main interest is not in the physical facts of the affair but in its atmosphere and in the effect of those facts on the minds and hearts of the characters involved, or in the state of mind conditioning the facts. In a strictly chronological narrative the reader is not let into the affair in its completeness until the end ; he is, being human, kept perpetually on the jump wondering what in *fact* will happen next ; so much so, indeed, that some of his attention is distracted from consideration of the thoughts, sensations, motives and what not of the characters by the purely superficial matter of physical suspense. Naturally not all action demands this treatment. There are two kinds of action in a novel : action committed by the protagonists and action befalling them. The action committed by a character is plainly a primary interest, and it is not always helpful to give it away in advance ; it is through his action that the character will be revealed to us, and it is necessary at times to lead up to it gradually, as the character himself leads up to it. An example of this kind of action is Nostromo's theft of the silver. But there are also in Conrad frequent important and in themselves exciting incidents contributary to the main affair and to some extent shaping it. And this is the kind of action that is best dealt with rapidly, recorded and put out of the way at the beginning, so that the reader can give all his attention to the minds of the actors in the affair. An example of this is the revolution in Sulaco. Further examples may be found at the beginning of " Victory " and of " Under Western Eyes."

But this is a side-issue. The main thing is the use of the broken method for an increased richness of texture, for allowing the parts to be bathed suggestively in the light of the whole. Of this process Conrad was a past master, and he brought it to perfection in " Chance," where there is no beginning and no end, and where the whole affair is under our noses from first to last.

The trouble about the novel generally, about all art which extends in time as well as in space, is that the reader is bound to be too exclusively in the present ; the more absorbed he is, the more wrapped up he will be in the particular paragraph he is reading, and correspondingly more forgetful of what he has already read and more un-speculative about what is to come. Yet the significance of a book is the whole book. The novelist is out to illuminate an affair, and if the reader until the last moment is unaware of the precise nature of the affair which started the novelist off, a hundred significant points will go for nothing simply because they must be related to a whole which the novelist has in his mind but of which the reader is ignorant.

There are various methods of relating the whole to the part, the past and the future to the present ; and since these phrases are vague and uncertain I will take an excessively simple example of what I mean not from Conrad but from a novel by Ford Madox Ford. Here it is simply a matter of a recurrent phrase, a device that has been also exploited by the cinema. In the novel " Some do not " that title phrase is itself employed on some half a dozen occasions within the narrative to bring the image of the past vividly into the present and also to cloud the present with a vague, uncertain foretaste of the future. " Some rest on snowy bosoms ; some do not," that is the key-phrase ; and every time a character is made to say " Some do—and some do not " there flood into the reader's consciousness images of past scenes where the phrase has also been the significant motive ; and at the same time its reiteration has a ring of ominous prophecy . . . it is becoming ever plainer that the hero of the book—does not.

That is an example almost frivolous in its simplicity, and it is to be hoped that any reader unfortunate enough never to have come across the novels of Mr. Ford will not take it as a fair sample of his technical ingenuity. I use it because it does provide what Conrad never provides—a simple, straightforward, and quotable instance of the effect I am

174

trying to discuss. When that device is elaborated and ramified almost beyond conception, as it is in certain novels both of Ford's and Conrad's, we have, to return to our facile musical analogy, the novelist's equivalent of the fugue in which the subject, or subjects, are with the listener from beginning to end, and where the interest derives from the pattern made by the changing juxtaposition of the subjects, themselves thoroughly explored and turned inside out. Reading " Chance " one may have the feeling that one is contemplating the rays thrown out by an active nucleus, the sun, shall we say, and by spectroscopic means analysing those multitudinous rays, arriving thereby at a precise knowledge of the constituents of the nucleus of fact itself, the sun, the affair, manifest to the naked eye only as light and not as a solid body. It is an effect found only in art of extreme maturity. To achieve it Beethoven in his later days was driven to extend the variation form into what we have in the " Diabelli Variations " and the last piano sonata, was driven in earlier days to the flexibility and freedom of action granted by his *quasi una fantasia* form, was driven ultimately and transcendentally to the great fugue of the B flat quartet. It is expressive of the conviction that all things are significant only in so far as they are related to a central core, a core which cannot be contemplated directly since it is impalpable, which can only be known through a minute and delicate study of its emanations related constantly to a something unexpressed save through them alone, the nucleus from which they spring. . . . And how is this nucleus in a work which extends in time to be kept unremittingly under observation ? How indeed ? . . . The answer, or the best answers to date which have been vouchsafed to that question, are certain works of Beethoven, certain works of Berlioz, certain works of Sibelius, certain works of Conrad, and, possibly, certain works of William Faulkner. It will be noticed that the musicians lead the van by something like a hundred years. I must apologize for dragging music into this, but because of its " magic suggestiveness " it was bound to lead the van in a form of art the goal of which, whether consciously realized or not, is the suggestion of the inexpressible. The hero of the piece, it seems to me, is Berlioz. Beethoven in some of his later works made music stand still by adapting existing forms. Berlioz forged a new technique to this end. His strange, his unique horizontal technique (for it was horizontal, although the richness of his orchestration on occasion has given rise to the almost universal misconception that he is a vertical composer, *i.e.* a harmonic as distinct from a contrapuntal composer), involving the use of a peculiar and apparently indeterminate melodic line, is fundamentally an attempt to encompass the truth he is trying to express in its remotest ramifications without ever vulgarizing it by giving what is impalpable a palpable symbol—a subject, in the musical sense. His heard melodies do not form the subject but suggest it, just as a contour line on a map suggests a hill. And the truth he is trying to express is, in this music, an unseen centre of gravity the nature and location of which is suggested by implication—just as the widening ripples on the surface of a pond indicate by their disposition the place where the stone struck the water, the size of the stone, and the depth of the pool.

It is possible that an idea has never been worse expressed

than that; but it is also possible that there was never an idea more inexpressible. The impulse towards this form of expression is essentially a modern impulse, and Sibelius, a composer sufficiently inferior to both Beethoven and Berlioz, has plainly been working towards it. In his Seventh Symphony he achieves it and time stands still. Conrad, in the novel, achieved it at any rate in " Chance," in which all that is visible and actual and palpable is in fact a shadow of the invisible reality, the inner truth expressed by the panoply of external phenomena. It is plain that in this field subjectivity is rampant. The perception of an invisible reality is bound to be exclusively subjective, and only artists of a sensibility extremely subjective will indulge in this particular form of exercise. We have seen how Henry James was worried by the compromising of objectivity in " Chance," how, nevertheless, he admitted that Conrad with his left hand gave back enough to compensate for what his right hand took away. He gave *himself,* said Henry James, a little vaguely. What he gave, in fact, was, by implication, a perception, a subjective perception of the unique force from which all natural action springs. The title itself seems not without significance.

Leaving the transcendental to look after itself, we can with relief return to the first effect of this broken method, which when used subtly results in an enrichment of the texture of the narrative. In the foregoing paragraph we have been contemplating somewhat moonily what might possibly be a second effect. With the first we are on safer ground, much safer. And this enriched texture, this reinforced density, this supercharged effect gained by making every word and every episode do the work of a dozen, is an extremely important aspect of Conrad's work. The only satisfactory way to explore its implications is to dissect a whole novel in detail, a process which would result in a book quite five times the length of the novel itself. But if the proper way is out of the question we can at least glance at the same principle at work in matters of detail, for very often a chapter of Conrad proves to be a microcosm of the book containing it. The sort of thing I am driving at, in this instance pleasingly free from all suggestion of metaphysical significance, is illustrated very well in the opening chapters of " Nostromo " and in the early scene between Mills, Blunt, and M. George in " The Arrow of Gold."

The ostensible purpose of " Nostromo " is to tell the story of Nostromo's self-inflicted ruin. But there is more to it than that. There is the tale of the birth of the new republic after the separatist revolution ; the tale of the married life of Charles and Emilia Gould, which is itself inseparable from the tale of the mine ; there is the tale of Martin Decoud and Antonia ; there are the tales of Don José Avellanos, Dr. Monygham, and the old Italian patriot and his family. All these tales and others besides are fused together as a framework for Conrad's revelation of the complex life of human society as crystallized in that obscure South American Republic, and for his study of " the passions of men short-sighted in good and evil." That phrase is the book ; the idea of it is the nucleus, analogous to the less easily apprehensible nucleus of " Chance."

In face of all this Conrad has the appalling task of setting the ball rolling. The book is a study in " the passions of men, etc." All these separate tales and destinies are illustrative of and subordinate to that study, which means that they must never be treated for their own sakes. And *that* means that they must be treated simultaneously, for if they are not, if we have one long section on this character, another on that, we shall become engrossed in the part to the detriment of the whole. Nothing in the book must be treated for its own sake, yet every character is real, every episode actual, and each thread self-supporting, real and not symbolic. And that is counterpoint. The various subjects in a fugue are never treated for their own sakes, yet all are capable of infinite extension. In face of this the ball must be set rolling.

Anybody can start a ball rolling, or, better than that, anybody can make a first move in a game of chess. But Conrad did not want to make a move for the sake of motion. He had to leave himself in a favourable position for future moves. In the strict chronological method his task would have been easy and the result unreadable. He would have begun with a brief history of Costaguana and Sulaco, following that up with a portrait of the elder Gould oppressed by the pernicious concession and dying of his worry. Then there would come a voyage to Europe to watch Charles Gould getting himself engaged and resolving to conquer the thing that had defeated his father. Back again then to Sulaco to find the money for opening up the mine. At this point our chronological narrator would find it necessary to take a bird's-eye view of things—a brief survey of the town, introducing a few other characters, Nostromo himself say, Dr. Monygham, old Viola, the

Avellanos, Captain Mitchell (though in this rendering he would really be out of place). After that a description of the foundation and working of the mine. After that an excursion into politics to indicate the unstable state of the country. . . . And so on, to a hard-won end.

That is the sort of thing that would have happened had " Nostromo " been written in accordance with chronology ; and the reader would still not be in possession of many extremely important facts after two or three hundred pages of it.

Conrad eschewed this method. Eschewed, I think, is the word. But eschewing the strictly chronological narrative does not take us to Conrad's final achievement. Great liberties could have been taken with the chronology of that story without any approach to Conrad's ultimate compression. That compression is cinematographic.

We glanced a moment ago at a device used by Mr. Ford which is also used by makers of films. It is nowadays a common thing to read that this or that novelist has borrowed certain devices from the cinema, and it is generally true enough. We also hear a great deal about the art of *montage* or cutting (an admirable art, to which all praise is due), that art which obviates monotony, heightens suspense, and shows a given subject from various angles of vision, which strengthens the film by enriching its texture, which affords freely the brilliant delight of contrast and which brings into the space of a few moments of time a significant juxtaposition of aspects and scenes. But not all the theorizing of Pudovkin, not all the cinematographic examples he can offer, can surpass the astounding jig-saw comprehensiveness of the panorama of nature, people, and events provided by Conrad in the opening chapters of "Nostromo," a novel written just after the turn of the century when the cinema was still a wonderful toy, when Pudovkin and Eisenstein were boys at school in Tsarist Russia. These chapters have all the freedom and none of the sketchiness and jerkiness of the comprehensive cinematographic panorama of the kind well exemplified by Ruttmann's "Berlin." Long passages of them could be turned almost directly into terms of a film scenario, and the only reason for that qualifying "almost" is because even the silent cinema of the Russians never achieved the flexibility which Conrad achieved in an obstreperous medium over thirty years ago ; the talking-film, of course, is nowhere. Contemporary novelists may borrow from the cinema, but the cinema in its best manifestations might just as well have borrowed from Conrad.

As an indication of the detail work let us dissect the first chapter itself. It is about 1,500 words long, a column and a half of a daily newspaper, a mere column of leading article in *The Times*. "Nostromo," like a fugue, leads off simply enough with the statement of a subject. The subject is Sulaco.

We have first the statement that Sulaco was once under Spanish rule, and after that an image, the image of the orange gardens with ancient trees to give the double suggestion of an exotic atmosphere and antiquity. There follows the statement that Sulaco is a port ; an indication of its size ; an evocation of its latter-day business in the form of a picture—ox-hides and indigo. Then we have a fleeting evocation of the past, of the Spanish conquerors in their clumsy galleons, this same picture serving to establish the point that Sulaco lies on a great gulf and that the gulf is noted for its calms ; then an amplification of this idea in the form of a dramatic comparison of Sulaco with other harbours, reef-barred and tempestuous, the point being that Sulaco has been just as inviolable as these by predatory traders. And then, to end the first paragraph, comes the clinching image which brings the whole picture into sharp focus :

" Sulaco had found an inviolable sanctuary from the temptations of a trading world in the solemn hush of the deep Golfo Placido as if within an enormous semi-circular and unroofed temple open to the ocean, with its walls of lofty mountains hung with the mourning draperies of cloud."

In that first paragraph, then, of less than two hundred words (a normal paragraph of *Times* leading article), Conrad has given us without the least hint of strain or effort the general situation of the city, its present atmosphere of quiet remoteness, a significant evocation of its past and an image of its setting.

That image, while closing the sequence, serves as a taking-off ground for further exploration. We learn that Sulaco is in the Republic of Costaguana ; that this Republic has a straight sea-board, fixing it thus perfectly on the map ; there is a suggestion of the mountainous nature of the country. Then—a distant view of one arm of the bay followed by a distant view of the other and a far-away vision of the peninsula of Azuera with a general indication of its geological structure. There follows a closer view of the peninsula with an image to suggest its appearance from the sea—its lack of vegetation, its lack of water, and the reason for it, itself conjuring up an impressionistic vision of its aspect from close-to.

And then for the first time—"it is said"; that "it is said" relating the landscape and its population. The people are now brought sharply into the picture, their superstitions about Azuera serving to throw light on their own nature as well as on the peninsula itself. We have the first hint of something very human indeed, a legend. Then comes a statement of the nature of the common people of the neighbourhood, of their occupations and means of livelihood, and with them the particularization of the legend of the gold and silver hordes in Azuera. This fixes the place for us and takes us still farther into the minds of the inhabitants. And then tradition—the evocation of the past, the human past—the adventurers of centuries gone who perished there. And then a sudden high-light bringing us into modern times—a close-up, as it were, of the legend—still impressing the landscape on the reader's mind and at the same time indicating something of the more recent history of the country, still increasing our insight into the native inhabitants, and placing, for the first time, definite people in a definite setting, a dramatic moment which brings the dead landscape to life. It is all done through the legend of the wandering sailors which marks the enthronement of what is called the human element :

"The story goes also that within men's memory two wandering sailors—Americanos, perhaps, but gringos of some sort for certain, talked over a gambling, good-for-nothing mozo, and the three stole a donkey to carry for them a bundle of dry sticks, a water-skin, and provisions enough to last a few days. . . ."

And so on. The legend is continued until the whole countryside is peopled with unforgettable figures, and this accomplished there is a sudden change of viewpoint·; sudden, but not abrupt. We see the bay now not from the city but from the sea, and for the first time the great range of the Cordillera comes into the picture cutting off Sulaco from the hinterland. We have our first glimpse of the dominating Higuerota. Further aspects follow ; the first view of the Isabels, those three islands which are to play so important a part in the story, where Nostromo buried his treasure and where Decoud died, where the lighthouse was raised to be kept by the old Garibaldino and his daughters. We have arrived at them slowly, and apparently casually ; Conrad did not single them out for a dramatic spot-lighting ; we are aware of them only in relation to their environment, and they are fixed in our heads all the better for it.

And ultimately, the whole of the immediately relevant topography, the history (supported by legend and lent thus authenticity), and the native population having been in those very, very few words branded ineffaceably upon the reader's consciousness, the chapter rounds off with the ultimate revelation of the harbour itself, seen from the sea panoramically. It is a vista as finely prepared as anything in the gardens of a king and as dramatic. All this apparently discursive wandering about the landscape has slowly brought Conrad nearer to the point from which he can give us in a single glimpse Sulaco surrounded by its mountains :

" From that low end of the Great Isabel " (which we have attained by an imperceptible and smooth progress) " the eye plunges through an opening two miles away, as abrupt as if chopped with an axe out of the regular sweep of the coast, right into the harbour of Sulaco. It is an oblong, lake-like piece of water. On one side the short wooded spurs and valleys of the Cordillera come down at right angles to the very strand ; on the other the open view of the great Sulaco plain passes into the opal mystery of great distances overhung by dry haze. The town of Sulaco itself—tops of walls, a great cupola, gleams of white miradors in a vast grove of orange-trees—lies between the mountains and the plain, at some little distance from its harbour and out of direct line of sight from the sea."

It seems to me that this chapter is a self-sufficient masterpiece of expressive construction and compression. The topography of the place, its past, its present atmosphere, are all, as it were, got in in parenthesis between the close-up of the orange-trees in the first line and the dramatic panorama of the harbour in its setting—with the mention of orange-groves again to close the circle. There is not a sentence which is not doing double duty and which does not convey more than the direct statement which is its face-value ; and, for an example, the little episode of the wandering sailors (typical of what is nowadays a very familiar screen device), by introducing which Conrad in the first breath of the book proclaims his genius, does about a dozen things at once. It serves as a relief to the pro-longed strain of visualizing the landscape ; it brings the warmth of humanity into the barren austerity of the natural scene ; it provides the reader with all the information he requires as to the state, material and spiritual, of the natives ; the implied gulf between the immediate present and the very recent past suggests, subtly, that the lives of the natives are not what they were ; it serves to underline still further the wildness and aridness of the landscape ; it introduces very forcibly an atmosphere of violence and greed into the narrative ; it gives, and most importantly, an air of authenticity to the author's own direct statements.

That is sufficient to illustrate the point at issue, and it serves as a " detail " example of what I mean when I speak of an enriched texture and of the whole throwing light on the various parts. We have here seen the principle operating in sentences and phrases in the boundaries of a short chapter ; it operates also in paragraphs, in whole sections, throughout the length and breadth of the narrative.

A moment ago we considered what might have happened to the opening of " Nostromo " had it been written as a chronological history, and before taking leave of the book it should be interesting to turn from small detailed examination to the broader aspects of the early chapters taken together. The first chapter establishes the natural setting and the second, with no less compression, imposes the commercial aspect on that picture, and, through Captain Mitchell, the political.

The first thing we pick up is the jetty of the Ocean Steam Navigation Company, a particular point in the harbour, that is to say, which has immediately before been presented as a whole. Considering the activities centred on this jetty we receive our impression of the general aspect of the country's seaboard far beyond the limits of the Gulf of Calms, which is later on, much later on, to be important. Further, the contrast is made between the security and reliability of the O.S.N. and the insecurity of the country itself, this by implication. Then, without any dramatic jar, we have our first close-up of an individual. He is a highly significant individual, since he is to serve as the thread of continuity running through all the narrative and holding in his hand innumerable ends which would otherwise be loose : the Superintendent of the O.S.N., the esteemed and garrulous Captain Mitchell. He is got in before he is seen by a phrase arising from the contrast between the security of European commerce and the instability of South American politics—an easy transition from the mass to the individual. And once he is in, even before he is properly seen, he is set to work. It is through him that we get our first suggestion of an outer world and the relations of Sulaco with it, through Mitchell's words about the Superintendent of a distant harbour, words which reveal him to us as well. And now Mitchell comes in for consideration as a man, and in the process of getting him sharply focussed we have a first glimpse of local politics, a significant glimpse :

" ' Our excellent Senor Mitchell ' for the business and official world of Sulaco ; ' Fussy Joe ' for the commanders of the Company's ships ; Captain Joseph Mitchell prided himself on his profound knowledge of men and things in the country—*cosas de Costaguana*. Amongst these last he accounted as most unfavourable to the orderly working of the Company the frequent changes of government brought about by revolutions of the military type."

And that is the jumping-off ground for a little explanatory raid into political affairs.

Captain Mitchell, as yet unmet, has been given us— " Fussy Joe "—and with a smooth and imperceptible motion we are plunged into political affairs. The little dissertation on politics is clinched with an actual and dramatic episode, and to lend this authenticity it is linked up directly with Mitchell, so far the only palpable character in the book, who is made, partly in his own words, partly in paraphrase, to describe the revolution, the revolution which will later be found to form the sustained crisis of the story. And it is this description which brings us the first hint of Nostromo himself, just a name, a man of quality, but as yet no more than a name. There is no leering pause at Nostromo's first entrance ; he glides facelessly across the scene and the description continues with the emphasis on Mitchell. But we have his name. And suddenly that name appears again in the height of the related struggle and we have a first intimation of the nature of the qualities for which it stands. He vanishes almost immediately and the emphasis again returns to Mitchell and his description. And now the description is dramatically brought to life and made actual by his revelation of an old scar from a wound received at the time ; and the nature of the wound and of the weapon said to have caused it evokes a sharp image of the ruthlessness of the fighting and of the characters and habits of the inferior natives of the town.

It is only now, after Mitchell has, with his tone of voice, made himself a permanent part of the landscape that we have an actual portrait of him. He is the first man to be portrayed directly in the book, as he himself no doubt pompously explains to new arrivals in Valhalla.

On these lines we continue for some time. Through the next few chapters character after character is brought in, caught first in a characteristic pose or exclamation and afterwards got in at leisure. The characters are illuminated by the brief episodes, and the episodes, sketching in the

Nostromo's character. And this is effected by taking significant liberties with chronology. The shifting imperceptibly from scene to scene, from standpoint to standpoint, I have described as effortless and unlaboured ; and generally it is so. But in that particular and extremely important instance, marking the end of chapter two and the opening of chapter three—the transition from the scene recollected in tranquillity by Mitchell to an aspect of that same scene treated as present actuality—the mechanism does not run as smoothly as it should. This kind of treatment will obviously place a terrible strain on the author's powers, and with the opening of chapter three Conrad for a moment seems in imminent danger of cracking. In chapter two Mitchell has been handing out his revolutionary reminiscences. Chapter three opens with a direct view of that revolution in progress, featuring Nostromo himself in action, and for a few moments the reader is a little muddled as to whether he is supposed to be in the present or the past. The trouble is caused partly by Conrad's boldness of conception and partly because he gets the worst of a battle with the pluperfect, which, like the use of " shall " and " will," was never Conrad's forte. It is a patch of undeniable stickiness, and it does seem to me very largely to discount the effect of the preceding chapter, since the reader is compelled consciously to pull himself together, look round him and decide where he is—to make a new start, in other words, the other in effect having turned out false. But this little muddle, although it is a blemish on the face of the narrative, does bring home very strongly what I have been trying to bring home all along—the extreme difficulty and the insatiably ambitious nature of the feat which Conrad all but perfectly accomplished. Elsewhere the art is successfully concealed by art. At this point there is a flaw in the surface, and through it anyone with eyes to see may glimpse the nature of the underlying mechanics as well as the high finish of the concealing surface otherwise intact. It is here that Conrad's genius may be seen for what it is ; that genius which excelled in formal synthesis and lacked the power of psychological synthesis. And in discussing what may be taken as mechanics it cannot be severely enough emphasized that here we are not recreating or even analysing a novel ; we are simply gazing at certain aspects of machinery, ignorant of its motive power and unable to conceive the mind that assembled the machine. Once assembled, once in working order, we can see a little the way in which it does its work, admire its qualities, and question its limitations. But that is all.

The opening of " Nostromo " is particularly striking as a piece of construction because of the extravagant complexity of the narrative, the vastness of its scope, and the density of its population. But in principle it may be paralleled by the openings of several of the novels—the leap into the heart of the affair to get its colour and atmosphere, the focusing on individual, significant, or typical aspects, which imperceptibly merges with the narrative proper, which *is* the proper narrative. For when Conrad is in this mood there is never a moment of stillness or a line of static description. The characters are indicated as they run and by the way they run. " Victory," " The Arrow of Gold," " The Rover," " Suspense," " Heart of Darkness," and above all " Chance," are treated either in whole or in part in a manner fundamentally similar to the manner of " Nostromo." " The Secret Agent " begins in another way, and so does " Under Western Eyes," with a swift impression of the environment, spiritual and mental and physical, which conditions the characters of the protagonists ; for that is all the brilliant rendering of the assassination in " Under Western Eyes " amounts to, and that is certainly the rôle of the description of Verloc's Soho shop—a piece of writing which, as an evocation of atmosphere tied to a scrupulously accurate account of actual visible fact, is unsurpassed in the English language. This kind of beginning is more usual than the " Nostromo " method, but usualness is lost touch with immediately afterwards.

The early scene in " The Arrow of Gold " to which we have already referred is perhaps even more skilfully contrived, and certainly more skilfully handled, than the opening of " Nostromo." This is nothing to wonder at, since Conrad was twenty years older when it was written. I do not propose to go into tedious detail here, but if the reader is sufficiently interested to take up that book and read the first part, quite a short part, exclusively with an eye to the subtle and ingenious revelation of character, he will, I think, receive intellectual pleasure of a rare kind. The main problem is to get in Dona Rita, to make her a credible figure in the reader's eyes without making her a shade less extraordinary.

That is a nasty problem, too. How best to obtain the reader's belief in characters of extraordinary quality is always a nasty problem—always provided that the novelist has the sense to realize that the very mention of beings larger than life will send up the reader's eyebrows instantaneously, and that once up there is no getting them down again. It is possible that the problem set by Dona Rita's extraordinary personality was what decided Conrad to narrate the story in the first person singular, for the use of the first person, the presence of the author himself in his story, will always lend an air of actuality—at a cost. On the other hand the first person singular may have been, and very probably was, decided on for very different reasons ; the experience which forms the book was, like the experience resulting in " The Shadow Line," too near to Conrad's heart, too everlastingly a part of himself, for him to feel easy in the manipulation of facts with an eye to effect and dramatic interest. " The Shadow Line " is an autobiographical experience flung down on paper just as it happened. " The Arrow of Gold " may also be flung down more or less as it happened ; but, if so, nature for once proved herself an artist of a high order. For the working of Dona Rita into the narrative is fine art, and it is helped by the use of the first person singular—at a cost. The cost is best expressed in Mr. Lubbock's words : " . . . the man or woman who acts as the vessel of observation is always in danger of seeming a light, uncertain weight compared with the other people in the book—simply because the other people are objective images, plainly outlined, while the seer in their midst is precluded from that advantage, and must see without being seen. He who doubtless ought to bulk in the story more massively than anyone, tends to remain the least recognizable of the company, and even to dissolve in a kind of impalpable blur." It is that trouble which robs " The Arrow of Gold " of perfection and which weakens " The Shadow Line." On the other hand, from no other approach could Rita have been treated so effectively, and since she is the book the cost seems to be justified. We have this figure, larger than life, and it is necessary to persuade the reader into accepting her extraordinary quality : the problem is, how . . . ?

Plainly to introduce Dona Rita for the first time as an actor in a set scene is out of the question. Her greatness was less a matter of action and speech than of atmosphere or personality, as we say. And personality is indescribable. In an earlier novel, the first of all his novels, Conrad also had a girl whose unique qualities he was anxious to impress upon the reader. Nina Almayer was not another Dona Rita, but she was an exceptionally beautiful creature and she had an animal integrity all her own. Yet Nina never comes off because Conrad approached her far too directly, and even at times committed himself to *ex parte* statements as to her appearance—to speak of a heroine's " glorious and sparkling eyes " is not the best way to set about winning the reader's confidence. Nor is it a great deal better to describe such an individual, an individual of extraordinary qualities, through the eyes of another character in the story. This is a more common method of approach, but all the reader has to go on is the subjective feeling of a single person. Any *direct* attack of any kind is in fact foredoomed, since it is at once made plain that the author is seeking to impress and the reader naturally enough can see no reason why he should be impressed. And yet the novelist's effect must be got otherwise than through the speech and actions of the character ; his immediate effect, that is : for although throughout the narrative the speech and action will quietly do its work, there is no strong personality in the world who makes his immediate overwhelming impression by anything other than an impalpable something about his person.

All things considered, it is evident that the only thing to be done is to make felt the atmosphere or personality of the character before he appears, and that casually, with no apparent striving for effect. If this is done well, as soon as the character actually appears the reader will relate his words and actions instinctively to that sense of power, beauty, or whatever it is, which has been ingeniously suggested. And this is Conrad's way with Dona Rita de Lastaola. His method is the simplest and the subtlest possible, for he brings her in as the subject of a long conversation between two men of the world whose particular experience and scepticism have already been established. From them, from Blunt, we learn the facts ; the facts of her life, the facts of her effect on other people of various types. We learn also that both these men are in their separate ways profoundly impressed by her. And finally these facts, extraordinary enough in themselves, we hear through the ears of an ardent and romantically inclined young man who himself has never set eyes on the subject of this midnight conversation, and is thus forced to image for himself a creature whose life and personality will accord with the facts of the case. And thus it is that Conrad achieves his vague image, his radiant haze, the suggestion of enigmatic and mysterious power in a vessel of extreme beauty ; the image, in a word, not of a person but of a personality. Consequently, at our first meeting with Dona Rita, which is also M. George's first meeting, we are in a highly receptive state of mind very similar to that of the young man himself. And (this, I believe, is of extreme importance to the illusion) when for the first time she opens her mouth to speak, the very ordinariness, the very practical sanity of her words coming, as it were, from a haloed mystery (words which had they been delivered in a scene which had been unprepared for would effectively have prevented the narrator from ever soaring above the earth in an effort to suggest her atmosphere), root that vague image which we have grown accustomed to firmly in actuality, so that her personality, the idealized image, is no longer elusive and wavering but a vivid fact pinned to reality. Her first words are, of course, " I'm sorry I kept you waiting."

The long preparation for those words is beautifully contrived. In the beginning we have casual reference on the part of the two men to a mysterious " she "—mysterious, that is, to M. George, but not at all veiled to his companions. That " she " is made nothing of at first. She is evidently in a position to get things done, rather unusual things at that ; but this power is not yet referred to her unique qualities of person but to her perfectly ordinary if highly developed femininity. She remains essentially a woman among other women :

" ' You mean to say that you expect a woman to arrange that sort of thing for you ? '

" ' A trifle for her,' Mr. Blunt remarked indifferently.

piece, but entirely casually as one may discuss anything of interest which happens to crop up in conversation. And Rita's realness depends enormously on this casual approach, unaccompanied by a single drum-tap and to all appearances probably leading nowhere in particular. This way in which Conrad makes the most extraordinary character he was ever called upon to handle just crop up at a point nowhere in particular in the narrative is a beautiful example of the restraint of genius, and one which by less spectacular instances is paralleled a hundred times throughout the novels. The two men discuss her, talk round and about her for some time. But at first no definite image is allowed to appear. She is discussed just as third parties are discussed by mutual friends, their qualities standing isolated and in the abstract, as it were. And this casual enumeration of unrelated qualities is the very thing to set the imagination of a listener, an outsider, working hard to construct an image which will relate all those qualities together into an organic whole which will inevitably be an idealized portrait. It is not until many pages later when we have an idea of her history (the unimportant extraordinariness of this history serving to impress the extraordinariness of the woman) that we are allowed to see her plain in a clear-cut image ; and this, as it should be, is an everyday image. It is in a casual little scene in the park that she is brought suddenly and dramatically to life and given flesh and blood. Riding with Henry Allègre she meets Doyen, the ancient sculptor, and for the first time we know her now not as a mysterious girl but as a mature woman—the unnamed " she " who can get things done. By the time of the first meeting with M. George we have glimpsed Dona

Rita from innumerable angles. We have accepted her, if we are to accept her at all, and we are ready to meet her face to face on the terms dictated by the narrator, by Conrad.

But even now the problem remains how to retain our belief, and it is here that Conrad again shows his mettle in what is one of the most beautiful examples of subtle persuasiveness in all his work, persuasiveness achieved with the utmost economy of means—the many-sided significance of the wretched Theresa. She has many obvious uses in the story apart from what may be called her atmospheric quality; but Conrad's supreme skill is displayed in the way in which he uses this unattractive creature, Dona Rita's sister, to keep the feet of his extraordinary heroine firmly fixed on the earth by never letting us forget the blood relationship and by slowly convincing us, with an extremity of delicacy and discretion, that somewhere in the depths the two women have their affinities—a procedure calculated more than any other to retain and strengthen our belief in Dona Rita as an actual human being.

By straightforward narration Dona Rita could never have been effectively got in; that is one point about the opening of "The Arrow of Gold." The other is that Mills, Blunt, M. George, Rita's sister, and Rita herself are all got in simultaneously with the establishment of the prevailing atmosphere. The course which the action will take is already sketched in the preliminary chapter, which also establishes the technical convention. Immediately afterwards it is started in great detail—a detail which would be too slow for the reader's patience without that initial indication of its general direction ; and simultaneously with the gradual unfolding of the plot we receive an essential part of the past, particularly of Dona Rita's past. In other words, during that long scene in Blunt's strange room with its headless lay figure, its cheerless stove, its slightly sinister atmosphere of "*Americain, Catholique et gentilhomme,*" we are contemplating simultaneously the present, the future, and the past. That again is the sort of thing I mean by super-augmentation of effect, by Conrad's contrapuntal treatment, a treatment which in certain passages, in this chapter of " The Arrow of Gold " and throughout the whole of " Chance," seems to raise the focus of the story above the tangible and the temporal, seems to engage the attention on a plane beyond the three comforting dimensions and to suggest the fourth.

We find ourselves here in a somewhat cloudy region and we will leave it, for I am concerned with suggestion and not with exhaustive exposition. We began with a matter-of-fact aspect of the time-shift device, and we will close with another—the deliberate breaking up and re-arrangement of the narrative into episodes for purposes of rhythm and of dramatic effect, for slowing down and speeding up the narrative.

In his book on Conrad Mr. Ford discusses one aspect of this device, the *progression d'effet*, a fundamental principle of novel writing which demands that " every word set on paper—*every* word set on paper—must carry the story

forward " (we have seen how Conrad fulfilled this demand)
" and that, as the story progressed, the story must be carried
forward faster and faster and with more and more intensity." In Conrad the acceleration of tempo is always
visible and generally the augmented intensity.

It may be contrived, it generally is contrived in Conrad,
by a multitude of small devices having to do with the
rhythm of sentences and paragraphs ; but chiefly it is the
rhythm of the whole book that is altered, and this may be
done when a novelist is covering an extensive field, as
Conrad usually did, by gradually bringing all the tributary
streams into one broad rolling current, flowing straightly.
Thus, in " Nostromo " everything in the book, all the side
plots and issues, finally empties itself into the personal
catastrophe of Nostromo himself, which moves swiftly
forward, too swiftly. In " Under Western Eyes " the
moment of great acceleration occurs in that dreadful scene
between Razumov and Miss Haldin, when all the loose
ends are finally joined. Immediately after that we have
for the first time all the characters on the stage together, all
the side issues fused into the final, fundamental issue of the
book—Razumov's atonement. This process is emphatically not a *narrowing* of interest. When, after unravelling a
hundred tangled threads, they are finally tied up in a neat
plait, the plait is no less than the sum of the individual
threads ; it merely occupies less space in—space. By
bringing the scattered parts—parts scattered by the time-
shift device—together, the tempo is imperceptibly but
radically quickened. It has the same effect as the
development section in a movement of a symphony :
and, to pursue the analogy, Conrad very frequently

passes from the development into the novelist's equivalent of a recapitulation.

The closing phase of "Nostromo" is very like the closing phase of a Beethoven symphony, say the C minor. There is the same breathless acceleration of tempo as the end draws near announced by a tremendous crash, by reiterated crashes, climaxes followed by anti-climaxes, and culminating in Linda's lonely cry from the lighthouse.

It is very like a Beethoven symphony. But it does not end in a turbulent coda as the C minor does ; it closes as Beethoven often did in his piano sonatas on a mood of retrospection. The reader is not left suspended ; he is let down to earth gently, quietly, and with sonorous effect. We have one of Conrad's polyphonic closes (the phrase is Mr. Ford's, but it is the only one possible) :

"Dr. Monygham, pulling round in the police galley, heard the name pass over his head. It was another of Nostromo's triumphs, the greatest, the most enviable, the most sinister of all. In that true cry of undying passion that seemed to ring aloud from Punta Mala to Azuera and away to the bright line of the horizon, overhung by a big white cloud shining like a mass of solid silver, the genius of the magnificent Capataz de Cargadores dominated the dark gulf containing his conquests of treasure and love."

It is the arietta from the last Piano Sonata of Beethoven, the calm repetition of the inspiring mood after all the turbulence, the bitterness, the starry exaltation and the darkness of the infinite variations. We are back at our starting place, the unpeopled immensity of the overcast Gulf of Calms.

Again and again Conrad closes his books on this note—
" Heart of Darkness," " Lord Jim," " The Secret Agent,"
" The Rover." It looks an easy device, but I don't think
it can be. For its success depends absolutely on the
integrity of the dominating idea of the book   If there is
anything wrong with that, all the wrongness will be magni-
fied and crystallized in the closing cadence, epitomizing the
mood.   About this I feel a little doubtful :

" The blue level of the Mediterranean, the charmer and
the deceiver of audacious men, kept the secret of its fascina-
tion—hugged to its calm breast the victims of all the wars,
calamities and tempests of its history, under the marvellous
purity of the sunset sky.   A few rosy clouds floated high
up over the Esterel range.   The breath of the evening
breeze came to cool the heated rocks of Escampobar ; and
the mulberry tree, the only big tree on the head of the
peninsula, standing like a sentinel at the gate of the yard,
sighed faintly in a shudder of all its leaves as if regretting
the Brother of the Coast, the man of dark deeds but of
large heart, who often at noonday would lie down to sleep
under its shade."

That seems to me an epitome of Conrad at . . . well,
not at his best.   It is an epitome of the book of which it is
the closing paragraph, " The Rover," in which too often
Conrad seems to me to call on his maturest qualities, his
delicacy and limpidity, as the Israelites called on their God—
in vain.

But in the close of " The Secret Agent " there is nothing
false :

" And the incorruptible Professor walked too, averting
his eyes from the odious multitude of mankind.   He had

no future. He disdained it. He was a force. His thoughts caressed the images of ruin and destruction. He walked, frail, insignificant, shabby, miserable—and terrible in the simplicity of his idea calling madness and despair to the regeneration of the world. Nobody looked at him. He passed on unsuspected and deadly, like a pest in the street full of men."

And there is nothing wrong with the close of " Heart of Darkness " :

" Marlow ceased, and sat apart, indistinct and silent, in the pose of a meditating Buddha. Nobody moved for a time. ' We have lost the first of the ebb,' said the Director suddenly. I raised my head. The offing was barred by a black bank of clouds, and the tranquil waterway leading to the uttermost ends of the earth flowed sombre under an overcast sky—seemed to lead into the heart of an immense darkness."

This handful of quotations is primarily intended to reflect Conrad's manner of bringing a book to a final close ; but placed as it is in this study it should suggest other aspects of his work as well. We have no time here to go into a study of his cadences and sentence constructions because with that kind of thing one must speak either exhaustively or not at all, with quotations innumerable, not only from the author under discussion but from every other writer of significance. There are, however, cadences in those examples which throw light in profusion upon the detailed articulation of Conrad's prose, as the reader can see for himself.

But the arrangement of a book's end is an easier matter than the arrangement of its middle. With the end in sight the novelist knows precisely where he is and what more is demanded of him ; there are no longer doubts as to how much to hold in reserve, as to whether a spurt would be advisable at such and such a point, and if so how much of a spurt, as to whether such a spurt will use up too much of his strength, as to whether if he does not spurt now he will irrevocably lose his advantage—doubts which must torment him when he is still on the laps, as it were, never quite knowing how much farther he has to go and what he has left in him. The closing phase of a book is to the author as the entry into the straight is to the runner. At last he *knows*. . . . He can forget the gruelling task of flogging round interminably and hoping for the best ; and if he has anything in hand, as he should have, he can look round him a little and pick up his feet before putting all he knows into the final demonstration spurt—a pretty picture for the critical onlookers crowding round the tape and passing remarks about technique, having paid no attention to it at all during those grilling minutes when technique and technique alone has kept him moving thus victoriously.

The manipulation of the book is more difficult at the beginning than at the end, and more difficult, infinitely more difficult, through all the length of its indeterminate middle than either at the end or the beginning. At the end you spurt ; that is plain ; at the beginning either you spurt or craftily go slow. . . . But how long to spurt ? How long before picking up your pace ? In the middle, too far from beginning or end for any easy reference to constants to be possible, you are like a mathematician trying to work out an intricate problem with shifting quantities. It is there that mistakes are made. It is there that you decide a little more humour is called for and start up a rigmarole about Mrs. Fyne's "girl-friends," and then, discovering that you have humour enough without that, drop it incontinently and leave it flapping loose ; it is there that you suddenly panic about your illusion, and invent an impossible diary. It is there, too, that the rhythm gets out of gear at time, as it did at times with Conrad. He would put off a spurt for too long, as in "The End of the Tether" and "The Shadow Line" ; or he would produce it a shade too soon, rattling the reader, as in the third chapter of "Nostromo." But on the whole he had an almost uncanny instinct for the most advantageous disposition of his resources in time and space. "The inevitable word," writes George Moore of Walter Pater, "which has proved of so much use to critics in filling up columns, was not sought by him, he found it without seeking ; he sought the paragraph, and afterwards the page, and after the page the chapter. And the chapter was sought in relation to the book : the book was always in his mind. . . ." Conrad by no means always found the inevitable word, but the rest of that criticism is true of him also ; "the book was always in his mind. . . ."

But there are times when, in his struggle to fit the paragraph to the chapter, the chapter to the book, to make every word, sentence, paragraph, episode in the narrative do the work of half a dozen, an excess of zeal brought with it its own defeat. There is in "Under Western Eyes" an interesting example of this kind of lapse, where the broken narrative, as usual, is employed to enrich the texture of the narrative, for realistic effect (Ford Madox Ford's gradual revelation of character), for the simultaneous revelation of numerous aspects of the story, and for rhythmic purposes, including that element of suspense which is indispensable. Anybody who cares to glance at the first part of the book from this particular angle can see for himself how very subtly the material is wrought ; but there is one moment of manipulation which does not, as I see it, come off, a moment which is particularly relevant to the immediate question of tempo and suspense.

Razumov, very gradually, has arrived at the conclusion that he must denounce Haldin. In a flash of inspiration he makes up his mind to put the whole matter before his shadowy protector, Prince K. The ordeal before him is considerable. The reader, having been alone with Razumov and his thoughts for some time, is keyed up for a dramatic scene. Razumov reaches the palace ; he is admitted. The Prince, impelled by idle curiosity, emerges to receive him :

" In the hall, the front door standing wide open, he recognized at once Razumov, pale as death, his eyes blazing, and surrounded by perplexed lackeys. The Prince was vexed beyond measure, and even indignant. But his humane instincts and a subtle sense of self-respect could not allow him to let this young man be thrown out into the street by base menials. He retreated unseen into his room, and after a little rang his bell. Razumov heard in the hall an ominously raised harsh voice saying somewhere far away—

" ' Show the gentleman in here.'

" Razumov walked in without a tremor. He felt

himself invulnerable—raised far above the shallowness of common judgment. Though he saw the Prince looking at him with black displeasure, the lucidity of his mind, of which he was very conscious, gave him an extraordinary assurance. He was not asked to sit down.

" Half an hour later they appeared in the hall together. The lackeys stood up, and the Prince, moving with difficulty on his gouty feet, was helped into his furs. . . ."

" Half an hour later . . ." And it is precisely that missing half-hour on which all our expectations have been centred. And the events contained by it are passed over without a word. Why . . . ? The answer is supplied in the course of the next few pages. The two men, Razumov and the Prince, proceed together to the house of General T. And it is there, in the presence of the General himself, that we learn what has so far been denied us, the precise nature of Razumov's denunciation, the tone which he adopts to carry this appalling deed through. It is easy to guess at what passed at this point through Conrad's mind. The meeting with Prince K., although it was the first and decisive fruit of Razumov's spectacular conversion to patriotism, although for the reader (as for Razumov) it was dramatically exciting, was, compared with the decisive interview with the General, the man with the power—the power to hang Haldin, to make or break his denouncer, to grill him unmercifully, to take him as an accomplice turned King's Evidence, or to reward him for active patriotism—this interview must obviously be rendered in detail ; it is *the* interview, a scene from which anything may spring and which will in fact influence the future course of Razumov's life to its end. And yet it will be spoilt in some measure if the scene with the Prince goes first, for then much of it will be no more than re-capitulation of ground already covered. Thus it is that Conrad cut the scene *à deux* between Razumov and the Prince, ingeniously conveying the gist of it through the conversation of the two men in the Prince's carriage, and thus, delaying his climax, serves it up in unadulterated form in the scene at the General's house. And this seems to me one of Conrad's rare manœuvres that did not come off; either he should not have manœuvred at all or he should have manœuvred more radically than he did, perhaps taking the narrative straight from Razumov's decision to the scene at the General's house, and working in the antecedents of this scene retrospectively. As it is, the reader, and not merely the analytical reader, must surely exclaim at the bland passage of that critical half-hour. The unconscious reader will let out an " Oh ! " of cheated hopes, the conscious reader a muttered " What on earth is he playing at now ? " And such exclamations are fatal to illusion, for they signify that the reader has become sharply conscious of the author's presence, an author, moreover, arbitrarily withholding legitimately expected information for his own purposes. The presence of a device is patent, as patent as it is on the stage when the curtain rises to reveal an unnaturally placed screen behind which, the audience knows, somebody sooner or later is bound to hide. And that is bad. For although I have stressed the delight of watching the author at work, there are two ways in which this interest may be indulged and only one of them is good. Faced with one the exclamation is a sharp, affronted " Oh ! ", with the other an appreciative, lingering " Ah ! "

For a novelist should never let the reader see what he is doing until he has done it, or, better, he should never let the reader guess that he is doing anything at all other than the immediate task of the moment. The reader should never be *consciously* aware, indeed, that he is assisting at anything but the plain narration of a story. It is only when suddenly a new point is made, a new effect revealed, a fresh angle of vision adopted, that the mind flashes back to realize the hidden significance of words, phrases, interspersions, and their ingenious placing. That is the delight. But there are times, and this moment of " Under Western Eyes " is one of them, when the author looms up bodily into the middle of his scene, takes off his coat, rolls up his sleeves, and virtually says " Watch me ! " There is no delight in that ; but when one considers the extremely complicated construction of the Conradian novel the wonder is that this kind of thing occurs so rarely.

This part of " Under Western Eyes " seems to have been produced on one of Conrad's off days. There is nothing wrong with the writing as such. This, for instance, is unsurpassed in all Conrad :

" There was a coal fire in an English grate ; Razumov had never before seen such a fire ; and the silence of the room was like the silence of the grave ; perfect, measureless, for even the clock on the mantelpiece made no sound. Filling a corner, on a black pedestal, stood a quarter-life-size smooth-limbed bronze of an adolescent figure, running. The Prince observed in an undertone—

" ' Spontini's. Flight of Youth. Exquisite.'

" ' Admirable,' assented Razumov faintly.

" They said nothing more after this, the Prince silent

with his grand air, Razumov staring at the statue. He was worried by a sensation resembling the gnawing of hunger."

No, there is nothing wrong with the writing of this part of the book ; for a teacher of languages it is miraculous (the present writer has been one himself and can speak with authority) : even Conrad could hardly have surpassed it. There is nothing wrong with the parts ; it is their relation that is faulty. And that very passage which we singled out as an example of creaking machinery is remarkable for another fault yet, and that is the change from Razumov's point of view to the Prince's immediately before the missing scene. This is impossible. The narrator is the teacher of languages and he has no private access to the mind of the Prince ; the only material he has at his disposal is the material supplied him by Razumov, either in writing or by word of mouth. It is improbable that Razumov so much as gave a thought to the Prince's state of mind as he, Razumov, stood at bay on the threshold surrounded by lackeys. Even if he had supplied the narrator with the fact of the Prince's suddenly appearing and then with-drawing before ringing the bell (which is improbable, as the suggestion is that Razumov did not notice the appear-ance), and from this fact the teacher of languages had deduced the Prince's thoughts, it could never be more than guesswork to be offered as such. This kind of lapse is extremely rare in the mature Conrad and it is impossible to explain it.

Finally, since we seem to have our knife fairly into this book, which yet contains so much magnificence, it may be cited as the most complete example of a tendency manifest in some of the longer novels, a tendency towards top-heaviness, towards lateral extension in all directions and in minute detail, followed by an abrupt conclusion amounting at times to what is, comparatively speaking, a snap ending. It is a failing manifest in " Nostromo " and " The Rescue," but even more plainly here in " Under Western Eyes." The story is top-heavy because there is nothing in the second part to balance the exhaustive detail of Razumov's self-revelation in the first part.

Ford Madox Ford has attributed this tendency to Conrad's poverty, to the imperious necessity of finishing one book, getting paid for it, and starting another. And that doubtless is a partial explanation, as all who are familiar with Conrad's letters are bound to agree. But there may also be allied causes with roots deep in Conrad's temperament, and to me it seems that this top-heaviness may very well go hand in hand with those other aspects of Conrad which we have already discussed—his peculiar inventive and psychological limitations.

That he needed a significant affair to start from we have seen, and also that the affair is treated not for its own sake so much as a pretext for exploring the characters concerned. Without his affair, which must be dramatic, Conrad can get nowhere ; and perhaps we may liken these affairs to so many ladders, to the ladder which helps him to the top of the tower : in the ladder for its own sake he is not particularly interested, but without it he can never get his panoramic view. He climbs the ladder in a few minutes and turns his back on it for several hours. He does not kick it away, as he might, since he is an artist, not a politician, and he must have an answer ready in case somebody asks him how on earth he got up there. Also he wishes to descend in due course, to finish off his excursion in a ship-shape manner with no nonsense about it, not to leave it floating gracefully in air. He does climb down when the time comes, honestly and without deception ; but it is a rapid descent : the view was the thing, not the journey to and from it. In " Under Western Eyes " he starts from his affair and proceeds to view Razumov, the Haldins, and all the other features of that suggestive landscape ; and, that much accomplished, the affair has served its purpose and must be wound up with despatch. It is.

Actually in this book had the revelation of himself by Razumov been resumed after the reader's introduction to Miss Haldin, and before Razumov's meeting with her, the weight would have been better distributed. The first part ends impeccably with that mystic scene between Razumov and Councillor Mikulin, at the end of which the young man announces his intention of retiring :

" ' Where to ? ' asked Councillor Mikulin softly."

The rest of the book is the answer. But the specific answer, the logical continuation of that scene, does not come for another two hundred pages, during which we have had a great deal of the Haldins and of Razumov seen through the schoolmaster's eyes and through the eyes of other people as the mysterious friend of the gallant martyr to freedom wandering about in the revolutionary circles of Geneva. What is required is some more direct self-revelation following on the beautifully timed resumption of the scene with Mikulin ; *then* there would have been balance.

" Under Western Eyes " is a failure, but a failure containing so much greatness. . . . Such failures are not common in Conrad, so rare indeed that one does not even for a moment slam down the book in irritation ; instead one looks up and wonders admiringly at the fact that he, or any conscientious novelist pushing his talents to the limit, manages in face of all these myriad difficulties to get anything done at all. For the inertia of the human imagination is such that it is only the sight of a man giving way beneath adversity which can bring home to us the magnitude of his struggle. The instinct is always to applaud the battler with circumstances who shows the worse for wear yet still persists ; he who comes through apparently unscathed is hardly noticed. It is easy to see why this must be so : how, without knowing all the facts, can we realize the rigour with which a man may have schooled himself to stand assault ? The instinct is to gaze wonderingly at Tolstoi and not Turgeniev, at " Under Western Eyes " and not at " Chance " or " The Arrow of Gold," at the runner who collapses at the tape and not at the one who finishes as fresh as paint. It is the romantic spirit coming out in us, and the romantic is the man who soars beyond his strength. It is the spirit, in many ways admirable, which makes us look more at the gallant human effort behind the job rather than at the perfection or lack of it of the job itself. It is not good for art, for there the job is everything and the man behind it nothing. It makes for the glorification of the spectacular failure at the expense of the quiet success. For in art as in life success is never spectacular ; it is failure that is spectacular : success amounts to no more than perfect fitness. This romantic impulse in the heart of the beholder can never be subdued, but a little more understanding would give it a wider scope and a truer focus.

We have glanced at " Under Western Eyes " and " Chance," very cursorily in both cases ; but we should have seen enough to show that the problems Conrad was faced with in the one in no way exceeded the problems he was faced with in the other. He was not in either case de- feated, but in " Under Western Eyes " he is badly rattled. In " Chance " he is not. " Chance " is wholly successful ; fit, and therefore quiet. We have seen some of the specific difficulties he overcame there in our examination of Marlow. The failures in " Under Western Eyes " freely suggest a score of others. And if we remember the various points we glimpsed in other books, in " Heart of Dark- ness," in " Nostromo," in " Suspense," in " The Secret Agent," the successes there—and the failures—we begin to have an idea of the author's supreme triumph in making a great work of art successful all along the line. There is no creaking of machinery, no panting, in "Chance"; no tangle, no jeopardized illusion—just one or two slight blemishes to remind us that all artists are human, like the false start with Mrs. Fyne's " girl-friends." . . . Then how much more concentrated must his struggle have been—to subdue the material completely and to keep the machinery quiet as well. This is a sop to the romantic spirit ; in success there may be more courage than in the most gallant failure : but it may be seen only if trouble is taken to discover the obstacles which had to be overcome. Approached in this spirit a novel like " War and Peace " may seem no more remarkable than " A House of Gentlefolk," and there can be no two opinions as to which is the more perfect.

VIII

T H E qualities considered in the last two chapters are all very fine, but without a proper foundation in actuality they are vain. That foundation is the capacity to write. It is as a writer, as an artificer of splendid periods, an evoker of atmosphere, a translator of concrete phenomena into living words, that Conrad is chiefly famed. We all know about his prose ; everybody knows all about it, including those who have never read a word of it ; the reviewers have seen to that : it is rich, glowing, atmospheric, eloquent, superb. Scattered through these pages there have been plenty of quotations but scarcely a line reflecting the peculiar quality of Conrad's prose as generally understood. There has been no design in this. There are in Conrad certain purple patches, including some of the most familiar ones, in admiration of which the present writer yields to none. But a series of purple patches does not make a prose-style, which is no more and no less than a vehicle for the transmission of thought and feeling. Good writing is no more and no less than the translation of thoughts, feelings, perceptions, into words with the minimum loss of intensity.

The word " style " is badly misused and has several connotations. Mr. Lubbock has complained with justice of the insufficiency of technical terms in literary criticism, an insufficiency which has made the writing of this study unnecessarily difficult at times. To his complaint I should like to add my own, namely, that even the few terms we possess are used with no attempt at exactitude. Hitherto the word " style " has been avoided in these pages, prob-ably somewhat markedly ; we have spoken of Conrad's prose, never his style. Prose is what he wrote. Then what of the *manner* of his writing—of what is usually called his " style " ? That I beg leave to call either quite simply his manner, or, if must be, his prose-style, hyphened ; emphatically, though, not his style : *that* word for the remainder of this book (which is not much) I should like to reserve for something very rare in writing, a something, moreover, which Conrad did not possess. That, I suppose, is the limit. . . . Conrad possessed no *style* ? ! ! Well, no—but it shouldn't be taken like that. I have tried to make it clear, and in a moment I shall return to that superfluous endeavour, that Conrad was a writer of magnificent prose, and plainly, since he was a man, he had a manner, a style of writing, a prose-style if you like, *a* style if it really must be, and one of extreme flexibility, expressiveness, and interest. It is my personal opinion (I throw this in as a mark of good faith to show that nothing in the least derogatory to Conrad is intended by these remarks) that at his best he is one of the greatest writers of prose that the world has ever produced. But he had not style, *style*, without the article. . . .

The present writer is aware, perfectly, that he has no etymological backing for this position ; he claims instead the backing of universal usage outside literature. That the word derives from the antique pen he does not dispute, nor that it was later broadened to signify a writer's personal way of writing ; but outside literature to-day that same word, corrupted, serves a most valuable purpose which no other English word can serve as well : it describes a something that exists in every sphere of action including literature, and literature, which bore the word, alone denies it a blessing. Every person has a personal way, manner, or style of doing everything, from dressing to writing verse, but few persons bring style to these pursuits. Every woman has a style of dressing as every runner has a style of running, but only one of each in a million of each has *style*, unqualified. And so it is with writers. If we employ, as we do, the word style to mean manner or way we are left with no word for the real thing, style in the absolute. It is unsatisfactory to say, for instance, that the prose of Ford Madox Ford has a *je ne sais quoi* which the prose of Conrad lacks. It is also inaccurate ; it is not a *je ne sais quoi* ; what it is is quite plain : it is style, without the article.

It may be advisable here to declare that the present writer does not imagine that a writer with style is necessarily superior to a writer without it any more than a woman with style is necessarily a better woman than her sisters. But both are undeniably more pleasant to look at, and, other things being equal, are completer. Unfortunately, owing to some natural dictatorial law which seems to provide that no basket shall have all the apples, other things rarely are equal. I will not compare Conrad with Ford Madox Ford, since this is no place to engage in controversy about two writers of established greatness ; but we may perhaps take a younger novelist who has not yet reached his prime and is therefore nicely *hors de concours*. The author of " Defy the Foul Fiend," Mr. John Collier, possesses style. He is not a peer of Conrad's ; but he possesses that something which Conrad hadn't got. He doubtless possessed it when he was still in short trousers, for style is a thing you either never have or are born with. It is a beautiful gift ; one can imagine none more delighting. It will take a writer a long way, but you can get quite a distance without it. The writer had a friend, a runner, who was almost a great runner and who had style which made his progress beautiful to behold ; but it did not enable him to win the mile for Oxford from a Cambridge fellow with no more style than a grampus (a blowing, spouting, blunt-headed, delphinoid cetacean, that is). The writer attended neither of these Universities, so there is no bias in that statement.

Style in running is, quite simply, perfect action ; but perfect action is in itself not quite so simple. It means really a series of actions in perfect harmony, every relevant muscle pulling its weight and the irrelevant ones reposing. The runner with style should never show signs of distress, for no matter how tired his legs may be there should be enough freshness in other less exercised parts of his body to give him complete control over himself. He does show signs of distress at times, but this is due to the competitive element, which is inimical to style, for harried by that, the temptation to lose one's head is very great, resulting in a futile strain on all the muscles, including those which have nothing to do with running at all : the runner then strains every part of himself to the utmost, imagining that energy expended is work done, a feeling very like the one that inspires the ostrich to his vanishing trick. But the first thing that strikes the onlooker watching a runner of this kind striding round the track unrattled by a puffing competitor is the extreme ease, the indolence, almost, of his movements. He has a great deal in reserve, and even going at his highest speed he will always have a great deal in reserve, all those energies, indeed, which are not relevant to running. There is no strain. In certain activities the presence of style may take on almost an air of insolence. Kreisler is by no means the world's greatest violinist, but he is the only great violinist with style, and to watch him throwing off a difficult concerto which has caused the composer, say Beethoven, an endless amount of trouble to write, with the same careless infallibility with which he approaches one of his own Chinese caprices, or whatever they are, may sometimes irritate the onlooker. I said infallible, but it is not an axiom of style that execution must be flawless. Kreisler has style, but he frequently squeaks, whereas certain excellent violinists entirely lacking style never produce a note that is not true.

Beyond the statement that style in writing as in everything else is perfect action, itself a series of perfect actions in perfect harmony, it is difficult to begin defining it. Perhaps it cannot be defined at all, but it is possible to indicate some of its more obvious attributes and certain elements which must be present in the temperament of its fortunate possessor. Of these last the first is a complete and perfect instinctive knowledge of his own powers and limitations over and above the reasoned knowledge which all artists must have and to which each new work is a challenge.

With this instinctive knowledge goes an instinctive restraint; and this restraint is the begetter of precision.

This instinct, for the two are really one and inseparable, is extremely valuable and is possessed by most animals in their wild state, by some members of the general public, and by a few artists, little and great. Handel, for instance, had it, and Mozart to a scarcely less degree. Berlioz had it. Beethoven had not. Neither Mozart nor Handel ever show the least sign of getting hot and bothered, Beethoven frequently does. In a great artist this instinct is a crowning glory, but the possession of it cannot make a small man great any more than the lack of it can make a great man small. I added Berlioz to Mozart and Handel because his case is a peculiar one, and people will immediately point to the operas, like " The Damnation of Faust," saying that there the man has obviously taken on more than he can cope with, indicating a lack of the invaluable instinct of restraint; the point, however, is illuminated by this apparent discrepancy, for in those great and unequal works Berlioz is perfectly master of the music throughout; it is only in the welding of the parts to make an opera that he fails, and this side of his activity has nothing to do with musicianship at all.

It is the conception of precision that brings us to the root of the matter, and in this context there are two kinds of precision. I should like to call the one creative, the other objective. Both are important in an artist, but it is the first that the writer with style must have, and beside it (from the point of view of style) the second is of little account.

We are on very treacherous ground now, but it seems to me that the difference between the writer with style and the writer without it may be taken back to their sharply contrasted attitudes towards, or rather in face of, the subject rendered : this may be a concrete subject, like an apple-tree, or it may be an abstract subject, like a philosophy of living ; but since we are dealing with a novelist we may confine ourselves to the concrete.

In rendering an apple-tree Conrad will describe his own perceptions of the tree (every artist will do that), but to the objective image of his perception he is a slave. He contemplates his mental image of the apple-tree, catalogues in his mind its various attributes, selecting for mention those that he finds most typical and significant (this process in a writer with a highly sensitive visual faculty being obviously automatic and unconscious), and puts all his force into making the reader *see* those attributes so vividly that the picture completes itself in his, the reader's, mind. This effect is obtained by the studied use of words, a precise use of words ; but the precision is purely an objective precision, the words being slaves to the external actuality. It is the manner in which nine hundred and ninety-nine thousand people in a million use words with more or less ability and skill. It is the use of the word as a token, as a symbol : the thing is the apple-tree, or the writer's perception of it—a human perception of a natural object, in short ; the thing is the apple-tree and the apple-tree is the thing ; and the words in which the apple-tree is made visible to the reader are the servants of a fixed and predetermined image, which has nothing in itself to do with words and which exists independently of them. The words are called up to describe the apple-tree, which is thus, if I may be forgiven, *described in words.*

The apple-tree is the thing. Conrad describes it in words ; but with equal effect it might be described in paint. It cannot be described in music, but that is only an accident. There are plenty of things that can be described in music, in paint, and in words—a mood, or a rough sea, for instance. In other words, apart from details of expression, which arise simply because the writer's canvas is unlimited, Conrad, together with nine hundred and ninety-nine thousand people in a million, is striving with words for an effect that, had he been otherwise gifted, he might have approximated to in another medium—in paint, for instance. The words are tokens for things that have nothing inherently to do with words, just as coins are tokens for things that have nothing to do with money, such as sheep.

This would not be in the least noteworthy were it not for the fact that certain writers from antiquity to the present day have shown that words may be used not only as tokens for living verities but as living verities themselves. These writers are those who have style. And style in any medium is a use of that medium not as a medium at all but as an end.

That is another way of saying that the man with style is a born writer, while the man without it is not. But it is not saying that the born writer is necessarily greater than the others. He is simply a man who lives exclusively in terms of words, as the born composer lives in terms of music and the born painter in terms of paint. A born painter may be a spiritual scamp, yet anything he paints will have style ; but a great spirit who is not a born painter, yet who is driven to express his perceptions in paint because painting is the thing he can do best, will never have style. Rembrandt had not style, but Van Gogh had. Conrad had not style, but Ford Madox Ford has. The painting of sunflowers by Van Gogh is a creation in paint ; a painting of flowers by Cezanne is a sublime reproduction in the medium of paint of the artist's perception of those flowers. It can never, never be precise in what I have called the creative sense, and nor can Conrad's prose. For the words Conrad uses can never be more than verbal approximations for things that have nothing to do with words. There are moments, however ; and in scattered sentences, because no man is utterly and completely one thing or another, Conrad achieved style. The only example I can think of off-hand is, " The *Patna*, with a slight hiss, passed over that plain. . . ."

The other sort of precision has nothing to do with style but with good prose, as such ; it has to do not with the problem of what is being expressed but with that of best expressing what it is desired to express. We may study it by taking a single sentence, what may be called the unit of prose. In a perfect sentence a variety of forces must be balanced perfectly, and a study of this balance, or lack of it, will tell us a great deal about a writer and his prose. But a man whose every sentence achieves a perfect balance is not necessarily a writer with style, but only a writer of perfect prose, and probably a monstrosity. Conrad's prose is by no means perfect and an inquiry into the nature of the imperfections should tell us more about him.

In the first place there must be objective accuracy on the part of each noun, adjective, verb, and adverb—the black cat sat calmly on the mat ; that is easy, but it is not art, for art demands subjective vision. Thus, in the second place, there must be the reconciliation of that objective precision with fidelity to the subjective mood or vision. Thirdly, there must be harmony arising out of the selected words in combination, making the sentence. Fourthly, that harmony must be so contrived as to fit into the general harmony of the passage as a whole. Fifthly, the stresses must be so contrived that the sentence forms an integral part of the rhythm of the passage—all this depending on the manipulation of short and long stresses, consonants and vowels. There are other incidental forces, but these are the main ones. It is easy to describe an object with impersonal accuracy ; it is easy to describe it with unbridled subjectivity ; it is easy to combine words into harmonious sound and rhythmical sound : but to do all these things simultaneously is the hardest task in the world. Almost always the pull of one or other of the several elements is disproportionately strong, robbing the sentence of perfect balance ; and this pull in every writer has a great deal to do with the moulding of the writer's manner or prose-style, as distinct from style.

Let us return to our old friend, the random quotation from the magnificent prose of the teacher of languages :

" The landing was prolonged into a bare corridor, right and left, desolate perspectives of white and gold decoration without a strip of carpet. The very light, pouring through a large window at the end, seemed dusty ; and a solitary speck reposing on the balustrade of white marble—the silk top-hat of the great feminist—asserted itself extremely, black and glossy in all that crude whiteness."

Taking the second sentence by itself—how do we find that it fulfils our conditions ? In the first place the objective accuracy of the individual words. . . . As a whole the sentence has an air of dry precision, and this is due partly to the fact that a number of the words are precise, partly to the physical effect of the cadence, which is taut and spare, with no nonsense about it. But not all the words, I think, are precise. There are, for instance, two images at odds with one another ; one is represented by the word " speck " as related to the silk hat, the other by the words " reposing " and " glossy." A top-hat, I mean, far enough away to appear as a speck would not be noticeably glossy ; a speck is a speck, and that is all there is to be said about it : it may be a red speck or a white speck or a green speck, but it will not be a velvety or a glossy or a silky speck. Nor does a speck repose. A silk hat, on the other hand, does.

It is the " glossy " that is, from the point of view of objective precision, unhappy ; and it is easy to see how it comes to be there. It is plain that the narrator was aware of the hat as a speck physically, not merely intellectually (the " desolate perspectives " indicates that), and that the words " glossy " and " reposing " are used relatively not to describe the object as seen physically by him but to relate it in all its immaculate pomposity to its incongruous owner, thus getting in an ironic dig at Ivanovitch with a consequent enrichment of the texture of the narrative at the cost of verbal precision. In the middle of a sentence describing a scene from a fixed standpoint the narrator, in

226

a word, suddenly changes his standpoint and projects himself mentally from his station at a distance from the silk hat to another place from whence he can perceive its glossiness.

Conrad had a strong inclination towards this rather high-handed behaviour in face of the objects he is describing. We can find a further example in the famous passage from " Lord Jim," where the fixed standpoint is suddenly abandoned, this time with an effect that seems to me undeniably detrimental :

" The propeller turned without a check, as though its beat had been part of the scheme of a safe universe ; and on each side of the *Patna* two deep folds of water, permanent and sombre on the unwrinkled shimmer, enclosed within their straight and diverging ridges a few white swirls of foam bursting in a low hiss, a few wavelets, a few ripples, a few undulations that, left behind, agitated the surface of the sea for an instant after the passage of the ship, subsided splashing gently, calmed down at last into the circular stillness of water and sky with the black speck of the moving hull remaining everlastingly in its centre."

I am sorry that the word " speck " is again dragged into it, for it is an ugly word repeated frequently, and is, more-over, the German for bacon. But there it is ; and this time it is the culprit. The narrator's standpoint, and thus the reader's, has for a long time been the bridge of the *Patna* during her voyage across the Arabian Sea ; and then suddenly, without any warning, and at the climax of the mood, the standpoint is shifted to some point un-specified in space. To a man standing on the bridge of a ship the vessel does not appear as a speck. And here, to make the lapse worse, the image is not even accurate, even if it is granted that a narrator may suddenly project his mind from the deck of a ship into space ; for if he soars heavenwards for a bird's-eye view, as Conrad seems to have done, the ship may seem like a speck beneath on the floor of the ocean, but not, unless he keeps pace with it a thousand feet above, " everlastingly in its centre," as from the bridge itself.

This, as I shall try to show, is not the mean-minded quibble that it may seem. We are engaged not in running down Conrad's prose but simply in an attempt to discover its features and the causes of its imperfections, which are also the causes of its individuality.

There remain in our sentence about the silk top-hat of the great feminist the elements of harmony and rhythm to be considered. There is plainly nothing wrong with the sonority of the selected words in combination, and the sentence as a whole also fits well into the larger harmony of the passage. As for tempo and rhythm—the sentence is in effect a half-close. It is the end of the superb scene between Razumov, Peter Ivanovitch, and Madame de S., and at the same time the beginning of the minor, subsidiary scene between the two men after leaving the Gorgon's den. As such the cadence seems to me beautifully wrought. It has not the slow, polyphonic roll of Conrad's full closes, some of which we have already repeated to ourselves ; nor does it come with the sudden, soundless braking in full flight, as it were, of the Conrad chapter ending. It is, in effect, a strong modulation into another key, the close and the opening in one ; the letting down and the taking up ; the gratifying resolution of a strained mood into a new and vivifying one :

"... and a solitary speck reposing on the balustrade of white marble—the silk top-hat of the great feminist—asserted itself extremely, black and glossy in all that crude whiteness.

"Peter Ivanovitch escorted the visitor without opening his lips. . . ."

There we have the slow decline, the fall, leading to the sharp, but not too sharp, statement of the new mood.

In sum, the sentence shows us that all the parts of our condition are fulfilled except for the objective accuracy of every word employed. And this must be due to the exigencies either of the subjective vision or of the cadence or of both. It is not easy to write a cadence of this kind without a sacrifice of literal integrity. The word " reposing " is plainly conditioned by the cadence, and the word " glossy " too. It is also doubtful whether Conrad would have placed the comma after " extremely " had he not been intent on achieving that slowly falling line ; it is indeed almost certain that, however vividly he may have been aware of the striking effect of " asserted itself extremely, black and glossy " as distinct from " asserted itself, extremely black and glossy," the inspiration for it unconsciously sprang from the preoccupation with sonority, although once found it serves admirably also to intensify the ironic effect.

One might, in short, conclude that the words " glossy " and " reposing " were due entirely to the requirements of the cadence were it not for the fact that this would plainly be going too far and that in a thousand other sentences the same sort of thing occurs quite unmistakably, resulting from the superior strength of the subjective mood to objective accuracy—among them our quoted sentence about the *Patna*.

The sentence we have superficially analysed is an ordinary Conradian sentence, chosen at random. It is a good sentence but not a perfect one, and sentences of this kind form the backbone of Conrad's prose. In our example the weakness is the objective accuracy and the strength either the subjective mood or the rhythmic sense, or both combined. It is a good example for our purposes, for it shows the faulty balance operating in a sentence which is not badly weakened thereby. It *is* weakened, but it gains rather more than it loses. In other sentences the loss from the same cause is a good deal stronger than the resulting gain in impressionistic suggestiveness. Conrad did write perfect sentences, but not so many as one would suppose ; and what robs them of perfection is almost invariably the sacrifice of objective precision to what I can only call atmospheric effect ; and this is achieved by an extreme and somewhat blind fidelity to the subjective mood and vision coupled with an insistence on words as units of sound. It is this failure of objective precision which is responsible for the weaknesses of Conrad's prose, and it is the overbearing strength of the victorious impulse which is his greatness.

It is the mark of the impressionist in him, and in the prose, as prose, may be found the same impulses functioning which drove him into fabricating the complex and contra-puntal architecture which we have studied in another chapter. The switch from the deck of the *Patna* to a point in space, for instance, obeys the same temperamental law as the switch from past to present, from the reported scene to the actual scene, and so on, in the structure of the novels as a whole. There is no doubt that the prose frequently benefits from this flexibility and is enriched thereby ; but there are times, it seems to me, when the loss of clarity is greater than the gain of crowding overtones. To say precisely when and where Conrad oversteps the mark is a subjective affair for the most part. Some would say that the intrusion of the vision of the *Patna* as a black speck into an evocation of that vessel seen from her own bridge does not spoil the picture. But there are times when this kind of impressionism is emphatically overdone, killing itself by excess. It is really more than impressionism ; it is a super-impressionism. As I see it the true impressionist relies on the apprehensions of his senses—in writing, generally on sight ; but Conrad fortifies his senses with his intellect. In the sentence that we took for analysis the cause of impressionism is admirably served by the selection for mention of one or two isolated and significant aspects of the scene calculated to convey the narrator's subjective vision of it. It is served, to particularize, by the use of the word " dusty " to qualify the light pouring through the windows. That the light seemed dusty is objectively nothing but the truth ; it is only subjectively, however, that it is the whole truth. And that is impressionism. In the conflict between the words " glossy " and " reposing " on the one hand, and " speck " on the other, the objective truth for better or for worse is outraged. Objects there, and therefore words, are used merely as pawns for the expression of a complex subjective mood. That par-

231

ticular passage may be regarded as a border-line case, but in the following extract, taken from " Nostromo," and typical of Conrad when almost at his best, there can be no denying, it seems to me, that the illusion is badly flawed by a failure in objective precision consequent on an arbitrary shifting of focus :

" Dr. Monygham, going to the door of Viola's kitchen, observed this retreat marking the end of foreign interference, this withdrawal of the army of material progress from the field of Costaguana revolutions.

" Algarrobe torches carried on the outskirts of the moving body sent their penetrating aroma into his nostrils. Their light, sweeping along the front of the house, made the letters of the inscription, ' Albergo d'Italia Una,' leap out black from end to end of the long wall. His eyes blinked in the clear blaze. Several young men, mostly fair and tall, shepherding this mob of dark bronzed heads, surmounted by the glint of slanting rifle barrels, nodded familiarly to him as they went by."

I chose that passage because it is a splendid example of Conrad's dramatic quality of vision and of his instinctive ability to seize on a single detail of a crowded scene, *the* single detail which will give the reader in a flash the impression of the whole : " their light, sweeping along the front of the house, made the letters of the inscription, ' Albergo d'Italia Una,' leap out black from end to end of the long wall." It is this, and yet it also shows how Conrad refused to rely exclusively on his visual sense and sometimes fell because of it.

In the first place we have an unimportant quibble, which serves, nevertheless, as a straw—the imprecise use of the word "inscription," which is altogether wrong as a description of black-lettering sprawling boldly over a white wall. The word may no longer carry the literal meaning it once had, but its associations, either the association of carving in stone or of formal lettering, are completely out of place in that setting. The word is saved as far as the impression goes by the irresistible force of the image of the torchlight " sweeping along the front of the house." This subdues entirely the critical faculty, and before it is awake comes the marvellous and searing vitality of " leap out black from end to end of the long wall." The false detail is lost in the flash of vision in the darkness ; it is no more noticed by the casual reader than a misprinted letter ; but the attentive reader is conscious of a slight, a very slight, jar.

More to the point is the curious ruin in the following sentence of a positively superb image. The image Conrad is seeking, one imagines, is that of men marching in darkness, their figures shadowy, the whole procession in the light of the torches simply " a mob of dark bronzed heads, surmounted by the glint of slanting rifle barrels." The word " bronzed " there is, or might have been, genius : not only is it an accurate description of the colour of the marchers' skins, but it also has an association, a metallic association, linking up dramatically with the " glint of slanting rifle barrels." This, one imagines, is what Dr. Monygham actually *saw ;* but if so it is spoilt by the intrusion of what he *knew* but could not see. In the first place the physical impression of " a mob of dark, bronzed heads, surmounted by the glint of rifle barrels " is hopelessly at odds with the preceding phrase : " Several young men, mostly fair and tall. . . ." The two phrases are at odds because tall, fair young men are perceived by daylight, not by torchlight, and in a crowd at that. Either Monygham saw the fair young men, in which case he also saw distinctly the mob shepherded by them, or else he saw " a mob of dark, bronzed heads . . ." and not the fairness of their escort. In the second place the image is further complicated by the fact that if the torches really gave a " clear blaze " one imagines the rifles would have been apparent as rifles, not as glints.

In sum, although the passage as a whole has immense power of a vaguely evocative kind, it fails to give what it was doubtless intended to give—a clear and definite image. The procession was either well or badly lit ; but which it was one cannot tell because of Conrad's extremely personal mingling of things seen with things known, of awareness both physical and intellectual. And this time the loss of clarity seems to me undeniably greater than the gain in atmosphere. It is an example that could be matched by a hundred others.

Until now in this study we have concerned ourselves less with Conrad's perceptions of tropical landscapes than with his mind in relation to the external world as such, which is why so few of our quotations have been glamorous. This has been all to the good, since the arresting quality of the subject, where a tropical landscape is concerned, is apt to distract attention from the author's method of treating it. In all the passages we have quoted, nevertheless, or in nearly all, the translation from actuality to words has been, broadly speaking, true and fit ; and if a writer can give full value to his perceptions of the most colourless and commonplace phenomena he is a good writer : it will be no more difficult for him to render the exotic than the grey. The opening paragraphs of "The Secret Agent," descriptive of Mr. Verloc's miniature emporium in Soho, must have been as hard to write as any passage descriptive of a luxuriant jungle scene, sunrise and all. The amazing description of the *Patna's* interrupted voyage across the Arabian Sea is no greater an achievement than the amazing rendering of the dilapidated growler conveying across South London Winnie Verloc's mother to her penultimate resting-place on earth. The duller the harder, indeed ; for when a novelist is dealing out a series of highly emotive words to suit a blatantly emotive situation he may (as Conrad often did) quite well get his effect, or what passes for it, with slipshod work, since the words themselves, regardless of their niceness, will daze the reader's analytical faculty. In a literal rendering of a Soho shop-window every word must be true.

It is because of this that the selection of the purplest passages to illustrate chapters on Conrad's prose of "style" seems to me misleading. Once we take for granted Conrad's command of words, of the expressive word (and if we cannot take *that* for granted, then the whole of this chapter is falsely premised), no more is to be gained by citing stirring passages from "Heart of Darkness" than apparently trivial passages from "Under Western Eyes." The only extra thing we could learn would be the scope of Conrad's vocabulary, and although an extensive vocabulary

235

is to be desired other writers as good as Conrad have managed excellently with fewer words.

These celebrated passages, nevertheless, are useful because they high-light Conrad's temperamental approach to the subject to be rendered, which, although it has nothing to do with the manipulation of words as such, plainly has a direct bearing on the nature of his prose. The first thousand words of " Suspense " prove that Conrad was a great writer so effectively that the whole of " Typhoon " can add nothing to his stature ; but " Typhoon " is a good deal more useful than " Suspense " for the light it throws on Conrad's psychology. Granted the ability to use words, a purple patch owes its hue to the arresting quality of its author's vision more than to anything else. This naturally holds good for every phrase, purple, grey, or in-between ; but in the purple ones everything is slightly larger than life and easier to see. Such things once they are said take on the air of platitudes, but unless from time to time they are repeated they get themselves forgotten.

This is the kind of phrase, taken from the three-starred passage in " Lord Jim," with which Conrad's name is most usually associated :

" The young moon recurved, and shining low in the west, was like a slender shaving thrown up from a bar of gold, and the Arabian Sea, smooth and cool to the eye like a sheet of ice, extended its perfect level to the perfect circle of a dark horizon."

It deserves its three stars, but this, it seems to me, deserves no fewer :

" The window contained photographs of more or less undressed dancing girls ; nondescript packages in wrappers like patent medicines ; closed yellow paper envelopes, very flimsy, and marked two-and-six in heavy black figures ; a few numbers of ancient French comic publications hung across a string as if to dry ; a dingy blue china bowl, a casket of black wood, bottles of marking ink, and rubber stamps ; a few books with titles hinting at impropriety ; a few apparently old copies of obscure newspapers, badly printed, with titles like *The Torch, The Gong*—rousing titles."

The key images of those two extracts are : " The young moon recurved . . . like a slender shaving thrown up from a bar of gold," and " a few numbers of ancient French comic publications hung across a string as if to dry."

In both those phrases the words are true and fitting. The first example would be called " poetic," the second would not. Actually they are both poetic, without quotation marks. The cause of the pseudo-poetic quality of the first extract has nothing to do with Conrad, who is merely finding the proper words to convey a given scene as he sees it. It is his vision that is poetic in both cases, for it is not the choice of words which makes those phrases splendid (though the choice is necessary to the splendour) but the vision compelling the choice. They are not descriptive of the Arabian Sea by moonlight and the contents of a Soho shop by gaslight ; they are descriptions of Conrad's personal vision of these phenomena, which is another matter altogether, having nothing to do with style. The words are true, as they must be ; objective truth is scrupulously served : but the vital words are " like a slender shaving thrown up from a bar of gold " and " hung across a string as if to dry."

In each of these extracts Conrad has succeeded in recon-
ciling the objective truth with the subjective vision. In
other examples, as we have seen, he failed. And sometimes, very frequently in his early days, he could write this
sort of thing :

"And under the sinister splendour of that sky the sea,
blue and profound, remained still, without a stir, without a ripple, without a wrinkle—viscous, stagnant,
dead."

That is simply the description of a mood, not of a sea.
There the word as an instrument of precision is abandoned
completely for the word as a unit of rhetoric. A writer
respecting the rights of words, loving words *above all*,
could never have written that.

I am not saying, Heaven forfend, that Conrad did not
love words for their own sake or respect them at all. He
did love them, passionately. One knows it and one sees
it in almost every line. There are moments when he
surrenders himself with something of a religious ecstasy
to the rigorous domination of words as instruments of
precision ; it may be for a chapter at a time, or for a fleeting instant, betrayed by a phrase. There are such moments
in our famous purple patch : "The *Patna*, with a slight
hiss, passed over that plain . . . " and "enclosed within
their straight and diverging ridges a few white swirls of
foam bursting in a low hiss. . . ."

All I wish to say is that the lack of balance in the average
Conradian sentence is almost invariably due to a flight
from objective accuracy brought about either by the
exigencies of, or intense preoccupation with, a blaze of
subjective vision. In our earlier quotation from the

238

torchlit scene outside the " Albergo d'Italia Una " the vision is precise, but in the excitement of recognition the wording of the sentence as a whole is scamped. In the bit about " the sinister splendour of the sky " the image is not precise but extremely vague.

Nor am I attacking Conrad's use of rhetoric as such (how should I, when we owe so much to it ?), but merely trying to discover what conditioned it. It is employed at times with most telling effect, particularly in the later novels where a rhetorical paragraph, a phrase even, leaps dramatically from the confined and even meshwork of the prose with the effect of a Verey light. In the early books rhetoric is often robbed of its effect by its own excess. In the passage from " Lord Jim " it is also overdone, I think— or, rather, it overdoes the passage. For actually there is not a great amount of rhetoric there ; it is the scene itself that is so charged. And when on top of that we have Conrad's intense vision of the actual facts of the case, like the slender shaving thrown up from a bar of gold, there is enough colour, enough atmosphere and to spare without the supercharge of rhetoric. Yes, even atmosphere . . . that is what the rhetoric is for, of course ; to get the atmosphere, to get the feeling behind the facts and stimulated by them. But a slight touch is enough for this, and Conrad himself provides it more than once, notably in one of the phrases I have pointed to as ruled by the god of precision, " two deep folds of water, permanent and sombre." " Sombre " is an atmospheric word used there, plainly called into being by the subjective vision ; and yet it also expresses with perfect justice the objective facts.

Atmosphere, that loose and convenient term, is, it seems to me, the final key to the whole of Conrad's technique ; to his technique as a novelist and to his technique as a writer of prose. The striving for atmosphere—not taken by itself, however, but in conjunction with those psychological limitations which we studied in earlier chapters, limitations now cited positively for the last time. And even this is not enough—the striving for atmosphere coupled with those limitations : we must also add the lack of style, the fact, simply, that Conrad was not a born writer. It is only when we consider these three points simultaneously that we can begin to get a true idea of the heroic immensity of Conrad's achievement.

He could not invent ; and we have seen how the effects of this deficiency reached beyond the mere inconvenience caused by an inability to manufacture characters and incidents, how it drove him to externalize his characters when he wrote of them in the third person, as in " Nostromo," and how, finding this treatment insufficient in subtlety, he was forced into telling his tales through a narrator within the frame of the story. And the reason why the exterior method of " Nostromo " was not subtle enough for a tale like " Chance " was simply because he was concerned less with incidents and actions and events than with their inner truth, an impalpable matter only to be conveyed by bathing those incidents and events in the haze of their own atmosphere, subjectively apprehended.

We have seen too the endless pains he took to break the story up, to make every paragraph do the work of two, to enrich the texture of the narrative by mingling the past, the present, and the future. We have considered certain of the effects of this treatment ; but the final and ultimate effect is *atmosphere*—the bathing of the parts in the atmosphere of the whole.

And finally, in this present chapter, we have seen how with good or bad effect, and at the expense of clear-cut line, he sacrificed objective precision to the subjective vision, changing his viewpoint even in the course of a single sentence for the sake of new associations, for the sake of atmosphere—as in our celebrated example he subdues the landing of Madame de S.'s house to the atmosphere of the charlatan Ivanovitch.

And the same necessity inspires his rhetoric.

The need for atmosphere is not unusual. Every great writer must have it (I hardly need emphasize that by atmosphere I do not mean that sense of physical oppression, usually called by that name, and certainly a part of it, obtained by Conrad by the use of rhetoric more than anything else in those early novels of the tropics, but, more subtly, the informing and all-illuminating mood and colour of a novel like " Chance," achieved as we have seen by ten thousand delicate touches). Many achieve it by showing the whole of the action through the unspeculative eyes of one or other of the protagonists, a way denied Conrad. But the happiest way of all is the way of the born writer, the man with style, who achieves it with words and with words alone. And Conrad, lacking style, was denied this too. The lack of these two gifts, one rare, the other common enough, placed on Conrad's shoulders a burden of impossible weight. He could not enter into the minds of his characters, he could not manipulate words as living verities ; he was forced to manœuvre with concrete images conveyed by words as approximations, a feat made possible only by an incomparable power over words as symbols and as sound. Instead of being a suggestive mosaic of words Conrad's prose is a mosaic of groups of words making concrete images, and in his endless struggle with the rigidity of images, examples of which we have examined, he sometimes lapsed into vagueness. We know his amazing visual faculty and we think of him perhaps as the supreme recorder of *choses vues*. But he is not that ; had he been content with recording purely visual impressions there would have been no difficulties in his way. He had the gift perhaps as fully as any man has had it. But he was the prophet not of *choses vues* but of *chose senties,* supremely so. And things felt are best expressed by words used as words. Conrad had not style, was not a born writer, and thus lacked the sense of words as words. Words for him were labels for definite conceptions and phenomena existing in their own right, and so the exquisite webwork of sensibility that was his mind had to express itself in concrete images, was for ever tied to observable phenomena. This explains his rhetoric, the attempt to convey a state of mind by an image subjectively laden and, as an image, really inexpressible—the use of serried adjectives, qualifying, qualifying, qualifying, and sometimes even cancelling one another out, the unceasing struggle to obtain by the use of words as symbols, approximations that is, a final and by this means unattainable precision—creative precision. And this dependency on the image of observed phenomena, it seems to me, may almost certainly be referred back to the unknown source of what we have most inadequately called the deficient inventive faculty, the inability to visualize in his own mind the nature of anything not apprehended or apprehendible through the senses—an inability which in this case robs him of style, simply because he could not visualize words as words, but only as the inseparable corollaries of *things*.

If ever a writer needed style, if ever one *deserved* the gift, that writer was Conrad. Had he been a born writer, had he seen words as words and not as fixed images, his task would have been so much easier ; for he aspired as much as any great writer has ever done to express shades of meaning and perception all but inexpressible, shades which cannot be stated but which can only be suggested ; and the prose of a writer with style is all suggestion. That Conrad very frequently achieved this suggestiveness, achieving a fluidity and allusiveness of an almost miraculous order—and perforce with what is really the most cumbrous machinery—is, as I see it, one of the most admirable feats in the history of modern literature, a feat which one may legitimately compare (without the least comparison of absolute merits) with Beethoven's feat in subduing and developing a medium into which he was not born as Mozart or Schubert were.

The born writer simply writes. He has no doubts and no longing glances for another province. He thinks and feels in terms of words, words which for him are the germs of infinite suggestion. But Conrad, denied this gift, yet aspiring to its natural end, had to write with unconscious self-revelation and indomitable courage : " It must strenuously aspire to the plasticity of sculpture, to the colour of

243

IX

F O R some two hundred and fifty pages we have talked about a great novelist without once coming to grips with his genius. It has been a bloodless orgy. And this seems to me as it should be. A writer of genius may in a passing phrase convey the essence of another writer of genius ; a critic may in a few pages of studied generalization contrive to suggest the spirit of a great novelist. But that sort of thing cannot be kept up for the length of a book. I have tried to suggest the way in which Conrad's genius worked, but the effect of that genius must always be a matter between Conrad and the solitary reader. This study is neither an introduction to Conrad nor a postscript, but simply a conversation started as one looks up with one or other of the novels open on one's knee, a conversation which because of time and space has to take the form of a printed monologue. Like most monologues it presumes a certain familiarity with the subject under discussion, and, again like most monologues, it touches only here and there, with the result that the listeners soon itch to drag this or that neglected aspect into the light. And the longer and the more complacently the monologue continues the sharper grows the itch, which is all to the good.

So much remains unsaid, but I should like to emphasize again that we never set out to discuss exhaustively any single aspect of Conrad's genius ; and if sometimes I have seemed to dwell too long on single aspects, it has never been for the sake of these aspects alone but for their significance in relation to the whole. That is why there has not been a series of labelled chapters like " Dialogue," " Construction," " Character Drawing," " Psychology," " Men," " Women," " Children," or even " Style." There is plenty to be written under all those headings, even " Children." . . . That is why, too, I have not attempted to " do justice " to the novels and the elements of which they are formed. Anatole France's definition of criticism as " the adventures of the soul among masterpieces," or words to that effect, is all very well, at any rate for a short space, if the critic writes well enough and has an interesting soul. It is especially applicable when an unknown writer is being introduced, his work rousing an emotion in the critic's breast which, described by him, may convey some idea of the nature and intensity of the writer's power. But a study of this kind must stand or fall by the interest it may have for readers already familiar with the subject and themselves aware of its power. . . . Such a book, had I written it, would have had a very different emphasis. In all these pages there has been no single mention of " The Mirror of the Sea," and that book, as I see it, *is* Conrad, reflecting flawlessly his spirit. But it is not the spirit itself that I have tried to examine here ; it is the manner in which that spirit is made manifest.

Certain things are unsaid, too, because they have been said before ; and although I have repeated things said in the past when they had a particular bearing on the matter in hand, there are a few books I have assumed the reader to be familiar with—above all " Joseph Conrad : A Personal Remembrance," by Ford Madox Ford ; " The Craft of Fiction," by Percy Lubbock ; " Joseph Conrad," by Richard Curle. How much the present writer owes to these will be made clear by the reading of them.

It may be thought that I have stressed Conrad's craftsmanship at the expense of his inspiration. The inspiration, for want of a better word, I have not attempted to assess ; to do so would be impertinent as well as futile. But the craftsmanship exists, and in case there are some who still dislike the idea of calculation we have the nature of Conrad's practical approach to art (as distinct from his theoretical approach, suggested in his prefaces and elsewhere) demonstrated perfectly by his own deed—his collaboration with Ford Madox Ford. Conrad believed in his own genius, but he also saw the necessity for craftsmanship in art, and no writer unconvinced of its importance would consent to work together with another man. Genius is born ; the books of a genius are made.

Conrad was not an unbridled romancer, but an artist scrupulous and conscientious, an artist, moreover, who, Henry James apart, has done more than any other English novelist to put the English novel on its legs. The method of Dickens was excellent for Dickens, Thackeray's method was good for Thackeray ; but as models for less gifted writers they are both of them abominable. The English novelist of genius has always been able to look after himself, but he has done little for the novel as an institution. Conrad has done much. Conrad and Henry James together, two foreigners, provide sufficient ground for the raising and flourishing of a vital school. Schools are bad for masters, but those requiring guidance can get it nowhere else.

We turned from the novels for the sake of this discussion, and such as have survived will return to them. These pages are not an attempt to contribute in any way to Conrad's greater glory. The glory is there, in the novels ; we have simply contemplated certain of its aspects.